EXCEPTIONAL LEARNERS

in Catholic Schools:

The Results of the Benchmarking Survey 2017

by Michael J. Boyle, Ph.D.
Director, Andrew M. Greeley Center for Catholic Education School of Education
Loyola University Chicago

Pamela Raines Bernards, Ed.D.
Director of Professional Development
National Catholic Educational Association

with Ann Kearns Davoren
Education Research Consultant

Published in the United States of America by the National Catholic Educational Association.

www.NCEA.org

ISBN: 978-1-55833-644-5
NCEA Part Number: RES-60-1578

Table of Contents

Chapter 1

Introduction and Rationale

We are a single flock under the care of a single shepherd.
There can be no separate Church for persons with disabilities.

> – *Welcome and Justice for Persons with Disabilities: A Framework of Access and Inclusion, USCCB (2002a)*

Framing the Context

Written almost 40 years ago, The *Pastoral Statement of the U.S. Catholic Bishops on Persons with Disabilities* (November 16, 1978) has served as a challenge to create a Church where all are truly welcomed. In an almost prophetic manner, the bishops have called for specific actions to widen the doors of welcome for those who are disabled. This call was not only developed for the Church but also for its associated ministries, Catholic schools included. Specifically, the bishops stated:

> Catholic elementary and secondary school teachers could be provided in-service training in how best to integrate disabled students into programs of regular education. The diocesan office might also offer institutes for diocesan administrators who direct programs with an impact on persons with disabilities. (p.10)

It should be noted that there are Catholic schools and dioceses who are responding to this call to open their doors to students with disabilities in increasing numbers. Anecdotal evidence suggests that there are exemplary programs across the country that have been developed to support the needs of students with disabilities. However, in most cases, these innovative approaches exist at an individual school level and may lack a larger system's approach that may help to sustain these programs. A coordinated effort to connect these isolated pockets of innovation would help to give voice to exemplary programs and offer support to a variety of faith-based schools. However, there isn't consistent data to demonstrate the extent to which Catholic schools are implementing these kinds of programs. Consistent data collection over time may help to identify these promising practices and provide a more unified approach to serving students with disabilities.

Past Initiatives to Assess the Field

In reviewing the literature, the most comprehensive investigation of the field of serving students with disabilities was completed in 2002 by the United States Conference of Catholic Bishops (USCCB). The study, *Catholic School Children with Disabilities (2002b)*, was conducted by the Center for Educational Partnerships, under contract by the USCCB. The study collected information from Catholic school personnel, parents, and local and state education personnel. The study (p.2) reported the following:

1. Catholic schools service special needs in all disability areas. This study reported that seven percent (approximately 185,000) of children enrolled in Catholic schools have a disability compared to 11.4 percent in public schools.
2. The Child Find process is inconsistent and difficult to access for parents of children in Catholic schools suspected of having a disability.
3. Catholic school children are less likely to be diagnosed with a disability by a public school's evaluator than through a private evaluation.
4. Catholic school children with disabilities appear to be enrolled in roughly the same proportions by ethnicity as their non-disabled peers.
5. Catholic school students diagnosed as having a disability are not receiving sufficient service through IDEA.
6. In the absence of IDEA services, Catholic school teachers, counselors, and administrators utilize innovative strategies for accommodating students with disabilities.

Additionally, the study noted that Catholic schools enroll a greater number of children diagnosed with hearing impairment or deafness, developmental delay, speech/language issues, uncorrected vision impairment or blindness, traumatic brain injury, or other health impairments than public schools.

It should be noted that this study was completed in 2002 and conducted prior to the re-authorization of The Individuals with Disabilities Education Act of 1997 (IDEA 97). IDEA 97 was reauthorized in 2004 and is now known as the Individuals with Disabilities Education Improvement Act of 2004 (IDEIA). Some may view that the procedures for private schools under IDEIA are even more difficult to navigate than the previous version of IDEA.

The National Catholic Educational Association (NCEA), as a professional organization, sought additional information about the types of disabilities found in Catholic schools to establish an understanding of the students who are served. Table 1.1 reflects these findings from Kealey's series of surveys (1996, 1998, & 2000). Though information regarding the average size of the schools is not available, thus making percentages of students served incalculable, the data does reflect that the number of students served remained fairly consistent during the time frame for which data were collected.

Table 1.1: Percent of US Catholic Elementary and Middle Schools Represented in Survey and Average

Number of Students with Disabilities per School

Report Year	% of all US Catholic schools represented	Average # of students/school classified as disabled
1995	8%	15 students
1997	9.8%	17 students
1999	5.6%	14 students

Source: NCEA Balance Sheet for Catholic Elementary and Secondary Schools (Kealey, 1996, 1998, 2000)

In Table 1.2, Bimonte (2004) & Kealey (1998, 2000) identified the types of disabilities Catholic elementary and middle schools reported serving, and the percent of the schools reporting they served students with disabilities. Bimonte (2004) found that schools enrolled, on average, 14 students who were classified as having special needs. This data remained consistent with the data provided in Table 1.1. He also reported that about one third of the schools indicated they had a paid resource teacher to assist children with special needs. This reflected a five percent increase from 2001.

Table 1.2: Percent of U.S. Catholic Elementary and Middle Schools With Students With Selected Disabilities

Disability Category	1997	1999	2003
Speech impairments	62%	74%	62%
Learning disabilities	66%	79%	68%
Physical disabilities	20%	20%	17%
Hearing impairments	25%	25%	18%
Visual impairments	16%	15%	13%
Autism/non-language learning disorders	5%	21%	15%
Emotional/behavioral	5%	21%	20%
ADD/ADHD	–	–	60%
Multiple disabilities	–	–	14%

Source: Bimonte, 2004; Kealey, 1998, 2000

In addition to the data collected at the elementary level, Guerra (1998) collected data from nearly 84% (1,015) of the U.S. Catholic high schools. In this report, Guerra noted the program offerings for students with disabilities, including specific reference to accommodations made for students with disabilities (see Table 1.3).

Table 1.3: Percentage of US Catholic High Schools Serving Students with Disabilities and Without Accommodations

Program Services	Percentage of Schools
Students with disabilities are served within the school's programs, but with no special accommodations.	37% (Approximately 375 schools)
Accommodations are provided for students with disabilities.	32% (Approximately 325 schools)

Source: Table 5, p. 22, (Guerra, 1998)

In another investigation, Bello (2006) reports, in a survey of 300 Catholic high schools, 94.4 percent of the 150 respondents served students with disabilities and other health impairments, which included students with attention deficit/hyperactivity disorders (ADHD; 79 percent). Other disabilities included emotional disturbances (27.8 percent), autism (9.3 percent), traumatic brain injury (9.3 percent), and moderate to severe disabilities (5.6 percent). Additionally, special education enrollment ranged from two to 150. Additionally, Huppe (2010) noted disability categories, such as retardation, autism, and emotional disorders, have a "significantly lower representation in Catholic schools than in public schools."

In 2015-2016, NCEA collected data on the number of students with a diagnosed disability in Catholic schools as part of the *United States Catholic Elementary and Secondary Schools Annual Statistical Report on Schools, Enrollment and Staffing* (McDonald & Schultz). Table 1.4 reflects the data collected from 2015-2017.

Table 1.4: Students with Special Needs Identified through the NCEA Annual Statistical Report

	2015-2016	2016-2017
Students with special needs	74,625	87, 165
Percent of students in Catholic schools with diagnosed disability	3.9%	4.6%

Source: McDonald & Schultz 2016, 2017)

Additionally, McDonald and Schultz (2017) reported the National Center for Educational Statistics (NCES) results that 78.4 percent of Catholic schools serve students with mild to moderate special needs. These needs include physical, emotional and learning disabilities that are accommodated in the regular classrooms with or without special resource teachers. The NCES survey also reported that 5.1 percent of K-12 Catholic school students had a formally identified disability, but may not have had an IEP (Individualized Education Program) or Service Plan.

NCEA and the Emerging Position on Disabilities and Catholic Schools

NCEA has long been committed to the education of students with special needs. In 1954, just 50 years after its founding, NCEA established the Department of Special Education (Behrmann, 1971). It concentrated mainly on supporting the work of dioceses and schools embracing special education, with a focus on day schools and residential centers (Weaver and Landers, 2002). Weaver and Landers (2002) noted the largest populations served in the schools were comprised of children, youth and young adults with mental retardation and varying levels of Down syndrome.

The Department of Special Education "offered professional services to those interested in special education in the form of conventions and institutes, the publication of a national Directory of Catholic Facilities in this area, a periodic newsletter, and consulting services" (Behrmann, 1971). The Department also advocated for and provided professional support to those who sought to provide services within the regular classroom setting (DiFiore, 2006). Msgr. Behrmann and Suzanne Hall, S.N.D.de N. served as the two Executive Directors of the Department of Special Education (Weaver and Landers, 2002).

Hall and Dudek (1987b) predicted in the Department of Special Education's newsletter that the role of special education would change within the next 10 years to become more integrated within the regular classroom. A 1986 survey of the NCEA membership indicated that the Department of Special Education was underutilized (Weaver and Landers, 2002), and the Department of Special Education was closed in 1991 (A. Dudek, a personal communication, June 25, 2001).

In the absence of the Department of Special Education, Dr. Robert Kealey, Executive Director of the Department of Elementary Education, published a statement on appropriate inclusion (NCEA, 1999) entitled *A Reflection Statement on Inclusion*. A former member of the Department of Special Education, Antoinette Dudek, took on the role of advocacy for students with special needs (DiFiore, 1999) as a member of the Department of Elementary Education team. In 1998, she authored the book, *Is There Room For Me?*. The book caused those at the national level to rethink how to serve students with special needs (DiFiore, 2006), while at the same time providing practical ideas and encouragement to those striving to serve this deserving population (Weaver and Landers, 2002; DiFiore, 2006). Its publication moved the issue to the top of the association's agenda, especially at the elementary level (DeFiore, 2006).

Directly related to the publication of the book, NCEA sponsored two national conferences on the issue.

> DeFiore (2006) notes the conferences were entitled *Making Room for Me* – clearly linking these responses to the challenge of the earlier question. They were held in 2000 and 2001 in California and Florida, respectively. Both conferences highlighted the need for Catholic dioceses and schools to address the issue of serving students with disabilities more effectively and presented successful, locally-developed models which others might emulate or adapt to their local circumstances. Presentations by individual schools as well as dioceses were made describing successful, inclusive and other practices in Catholic schools around the country (p. 457).

In the summer of 1998, NCEA's Selected Programs for Improving Catholic Education (SPICE) focused some of its effort on identifying successful local programs in this area (DiFiore, 2006). Among the programs identified were St. Thomas Aquinas in Indianapolis, Indiana; St. Peter Inter-Parish School, Jefferson City, Missouri; and the Mecklenburg area in Charlotte, North Carolina (DiFiore, 2001). In 1998, *Providing for the Diverse Needs of Youth and Their Families* (Haney and O'Keefe) was produced from the efforts of the SPICE Conversations in *Excellence Series*, with topics that included current social conditions, descriptions of award-winning SPICE programs, and pedagogical approaches to meet the diverse learning needs of students.

To further local efforts to support special education initiatives, scholarship grants for Catholic school teachers pursuing graduate study in special education were also offered. The grants were funded by the Catholic Daughters of the Americas and administered by NCEA (DiFiore, 2006). The Catholic Daughters of the Americas were committed to supporting children with special needs in Catholic schools, and the scholarship was a testament to their belief that knowledgeable and concerned teachers were key to successful school programs. This program was in effect from 1991-92 through 2012-13 and approximately 207 Catholic school educators were awarded scholarship grants during the time of the program.

In addition to the *Making Room for Me* Conferences held in 2000 and 2001, NCEA sponsored Special Education Conferences from 2007 through 2014 in Florida, California, South Carolina and Georgia. The name shifted from the "Special Education Conference" to the "Teaching Exceptional Learners Conference" in 2013. However, due to low enrollment numbers, the 2015 conference was cancelled.

Shortly after the special education conferences ended, the superintendents at the Catholic Leadership Summit in 2015 expressed a desire for continued support in the area of Exceptional Learners. Responding to this request, the 2017 NCEA New Directions Exceptional Learners Conference was held in Evanston, Illinois in June with a record 248 attendees, representing 31 states, the District of Columbia and Canada, 43 arch/dioceses, and seven Catholic institutions of higher learning.

Providing for the Diverse Needs of Youth and Their Families: Conversations in Excellence (Haney and O'Keefe, 1998) and *Is There Room for Me?* (Dudek, 1998) provided the foundation for additional publications to come on the topic of special education. In the years to follow, NCEA published 13 additional books. In 2017, NCEA introduced short-format publications called "Briefs." These booklets were designed to provide succinct and focused information on topics that K – 12 educators expressed were important to them. The three first books published were part of the Exceptional Learners Series and included Core Reading Instruction, (Lia, 2017), *Our Legacy and Our Future: A Framework for Serving English Language Learners in Catholic Schools*, (Dees, Lichon & Roach, 2017), and *The Meaning of Gifts and Talents: Framing the Elements for Flourishing*, (Boazman, 2017). Two additional books and two briefs are scheduled to be published in time for the NCEA 2018 Convention & Expo in Cincinnati, Ohio.

In addition to its publications, NCEA has provided support to its members on the topic of serving students with disabilities/exceptional learners through its quarterly magazine, *Momentum*. In 2015, NCEA responded to an increasing technologically savvy membership by providing webinars and blogs on this topic. Additionally, NCEA responded to one of the action items identified in *One Spirit, One Body: An Agenda for Serving Students with Disabilities in Catholic Schools*, to create a web-based repository to house and share school-created products (procedures, flow charts, and other documents) around the implementation of inclusionary practices. Shortly after the 2017 NCEA New Directions Exceptional Learners Conference, an Exceptional Learners Resource page was created on the NCEA website.

In 2015, NCEA created advisory councils to advance the work of the organization. Under the direction of Pamela Bernards, Ed.D, NCEA Director of Professional Development, an Exceptional Learner Council Committee (ELCC) was established and comprised of representatives of Catholic institutions of higher education, diocesan and school staff and corporate supporters of Catholic education. In its first year, the ELCC provided guidance on programming for the 2017 NCEA New Directions Exceptional Learners Conference and collaborated on the creation of the NCEA Resource, *Who Are Exceptional Learners in Catholic Schools?* This document noted "the belief that all students are exceptional in that they are made in the image and likeness of Christ and should have access to a Catholic school education," while at the same time noting "Catholic schools acknowledge that there are those students who require special services to meet their human potential. Because of their Catholic focus, respect for the dignity of the human person, and commitment to justice, Catholic schools are uniquely positioned to meet their needs" (NCEA, 2017). Additionally, the document provided a definition for exceptional learners in Catholic schools and outlined a framework for structuring local student service programs.

Connecting to "One Spirit, One Body"

In much the same way that *Is There Room for Me?* (Dudek, 1998) renewed interest in special education in the late 1990's, NCEA's publication of the white paper, *One Spirit, One Body: An Agenda for Serving Students with Disabilities in Catholic Schools* (Boyle and Bernards, 2017) hopes to provide the same kind of impetus for serving students with disabilities in Catholic schools and provide continued support in developing and sustaining programs for students with disabilities. The white paper, a collaborative effort between the Andrew M. Greeley Center for Catholic Education, Loyola University Chicago, and NCEA, reviews the Church's call to inclusion during the previous 50 years and offers a framework outlining a systematic approach to developing a comprehensive system of support for inclusion practices in Catholic schools. To continue these efforts, there is a need for updated data to assist with developing the systems and supports suggested by the agenda set forth in this white paper.

The supports and services that are articulated in *One Spirit, One Body* provided the general framework for organizing the questions of the Benchmark Survey (See Figure 1.1).

Research Questions

Figure 1.1: Conceptual Framework for the National Benchmark Survey

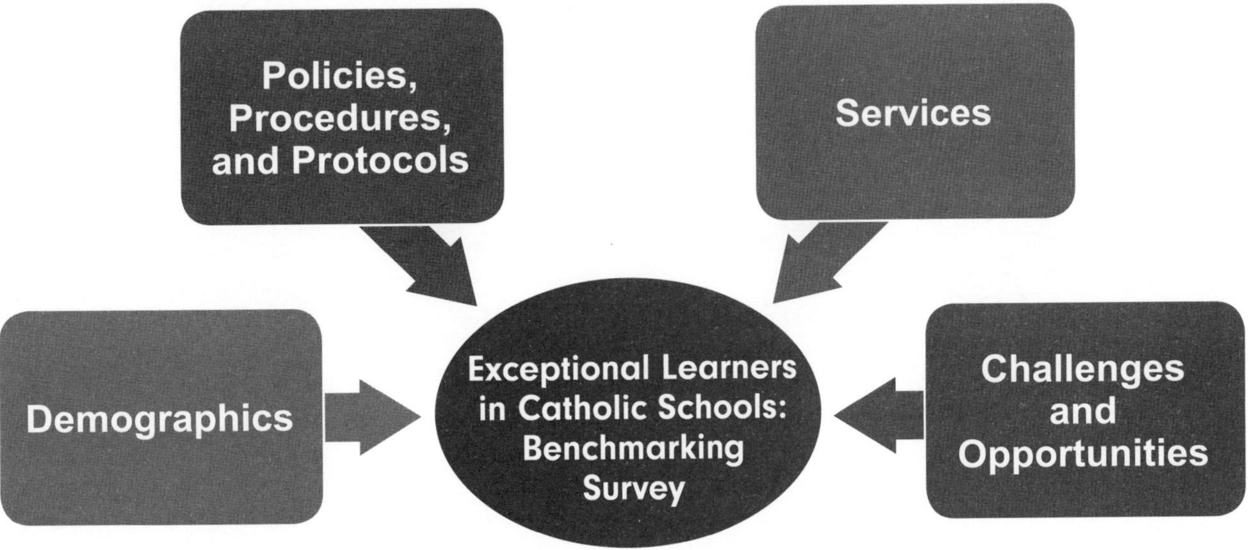

Demographics

Included here are the disability categories that are represented within the Catholic school setting. It is important to get a sense of the range of disabilities present in order to help identify the kinds of supports that may be needed to build the capacity of local Catholic schools to expand the offerings. The ultimate objective is to start to gauge the range of students that we serve in Catholic schools.

Policies, Procedures and Protocols

This group of questions was developed to explore the presence of the administrative systems and supports that are present, both at the local and diocesan levels focused on programming for students with disabilities within the Catholic school setting.

Services

This group of questions was developed to assess the extent to which students with disabilities are receiving supportive services within the Catholic school. This set of questions also sought to start to explore the connection between services and supports and student achievement outcomes. Additionally, this domain of the survey was designed to assess the funding sources that pay for these services.

Challenges and Opportunities

This section was meant to explore practitioner perceptions of challenges and potential opportunities. Here professional development and faculty training opportunities are being assessed. It is important to gauge the necessary kinds of training that are being conducted in order to assess what additional strategies could be implemented.

Chapter 2

Methodology

Participants

Using the NCEA data base, a general email containing a link to an online survey that had been programmed, using the online software, ***SurveyMonkey***, was sent to NCEA members. Additional follow-up emails were sent to elicit additional survey responses. The researchers received approximately a 30 percent response rate among superintendents and two percent among principals. More information regarding the respondent demographics can be found below.

Although the response rate for the superintendents was respectable, the response rate for the principals was not as robust as desired. There are several probable explanations for this. First, the comprehensive nature of the principal survey may have deterred individuals from responding. Secondly, the timing of the distribution of the survey (occurring toward the end of the year) may not have been optimal for securing the desired number of responses. Finally, this was the first time a survey of this nature was distributed. It is hoped that future respondents will become familiar over time with the nature of the survey and comply with the administration, thereby increasing the response rate.

Superintendents' Demographics

The 53 superintendents who responded to the survey represent 2,195 schools from across the country and over 650,000 students (see Table 2.1). Just over one-half (53 percent) of superintendents represent urban school districts; an additional 22 percent and 24 percent respectively represent suburban and rural districts, and two percent represent inner city districts. Just over 50 percent of the schools represented by superintendents are parish schools (see Figure 2.1).

Table 2.1: Number of NCEA Regions Represented by Superintendents

NCEA Region	Number of Responding Dioceses within Region	Total Number of Students Represented by Responding SI within Region
Northeast	5	102,486
Mideast	5	65,174
Great Lakes	9	157,963
Plains	10	103,375
Southeast	7	65,358
Far West	6	90,798
West	9	62,683

Figure 2.1: School Type Represented by Superintendent Respondents

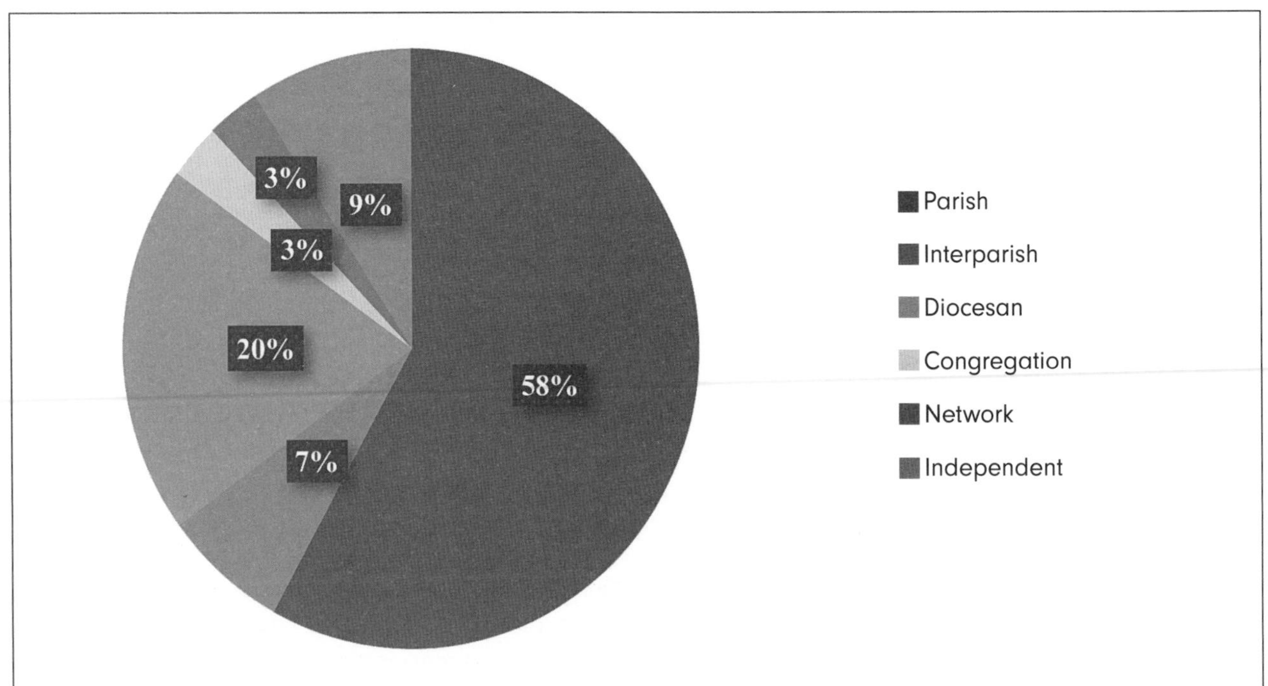

Principals' Demographics

Usable responses were provided by 119 principals. Over 25 percent of the principals oversee a school in an urban area, 34 percent suburban, 30 percent rural, and nine percent inner city (see Figure 2.2). Two-thirds of the principals are in a parish school, and just under one-quarter are in a diocesan school. The majority of principals who responded (70 percent) are in pre-Kindergarten through 8th grade schools, and another 17% are with schools that include high schools, either strictly high school grades or some combination of grade school and high school. The remainder are junior high schools or schools that service just the lower elementary grades up to 4th or 6th grade.

In terms of geographical representation, over half of the respondent principals represented the Great Lakes and Plains regions of NCEA (see Table 2.2). The remainder of the respondents were roughly evenly distributed among the other NCEA regions.

The total enrollment ranges from 29 to 1,230 with a mean of 275. In total, these principals represent 32,712 students. On average, institutions have a student body that is roughly 16 percent minority and 84 percent white; however, the range goes to the extremes with at least two institutions with populations that are 100 percent minority or 100 percent white. And, on average, about 16 percent of the students identify as Hispanic/Latino.

Table 2.2: Number of NCEA Regions Represented by Principals

NCEA Region	Number of Responding Dioceses within Region	Total Number of Students Represented by Responding Principal within Region
Northeast	9	2,784
Mideast	7	2,110
Great Lakes	31	7,245
Plains	31	8,267
Southeast	15	3,984
Far West	12	4,174
West	8	2,251

Figure 2.2: School Community Represented by Principal Respondents

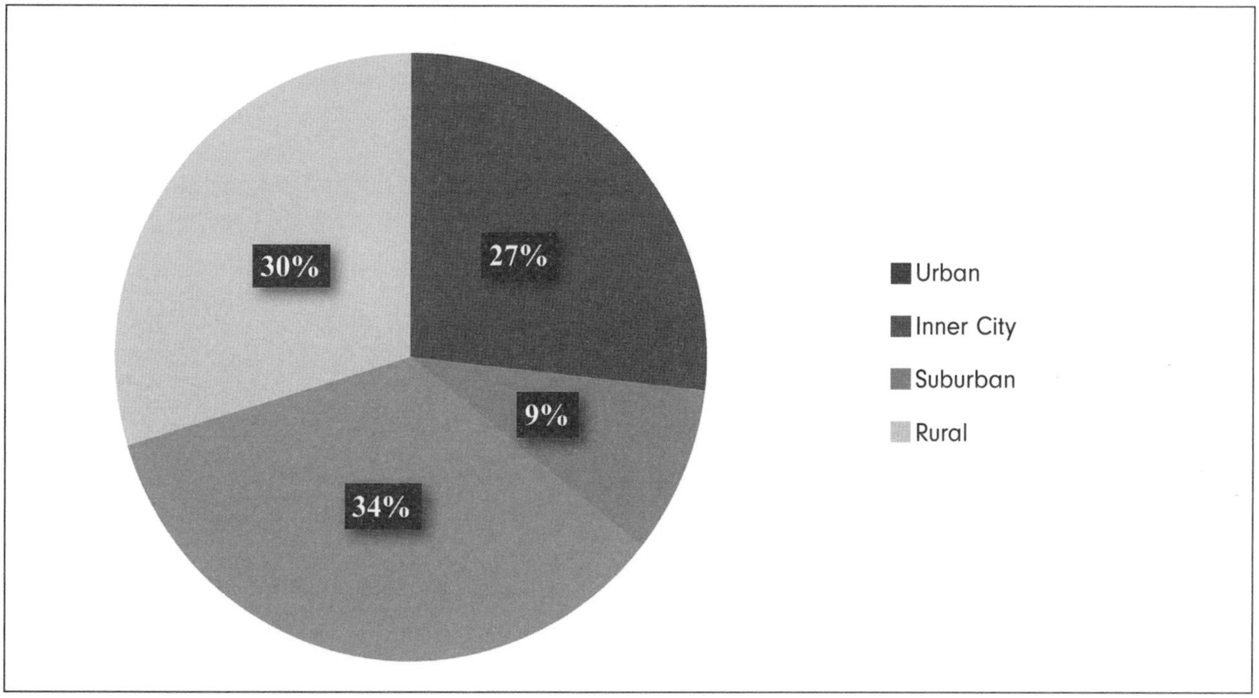

Survey Instrument

The survey instruments were created by an outside research consultant in conjunction with staff from the Andrew M. Greeley Center for Catholic Education housed at Loyola University, Chicago, and staff from NCEA. The survey instrument was developed by building on some of the original items in the USCCB (2002b) survey. Additional items were added to reflect some of the current issues related to serving students with disabilities.

The principal survey was piloted by several current and former Catholic school principals, and changes were made based on their recommendations. The superintendent survey was drafted from the principal survey and intended to measure many of the same concepts but did not include the level of detail the principal survey captured. The surveys were administered online, and all responses were anonymous.

Data Analyses

Descriptive analysis using IMB SPSS Statistics 23 was done. The bulk of the information was provided by the principal survey. Superintendent data will supplement that information where appropriate. Relationship testing using chi-square analysis also was used to determine if there were significant relationships between growth in reading and math ability among students with a disability and institutional policies and practices surrounding their disabled student population.

Chapter 3

Demographics: Whom Do We Serve?

Prevalence of Students with Disabilities in Catholic Schools

Rough estimates of the number of disabled students who attend their schools were provided by both the superintendents and the principals. Superintendents reported that the overall percent of their student bodies who are disabled ranged from roughly .25 percent to over 14 percent with an average of about six percent and a median of 5.5 percent. A few superintendents noted that their estimates did not include each school under their jurisdiction. Independent schools, in particular, were mentioned as not being a part of their estimates.

On average, students with diagnosed disabilities comprise 9.3% of the overall population (median is 7.1%). There is a correlation between the proportion of a school's population with a diagnosed disability and the proportion of the school's minority student population (see Table 3.1). As minority populations rise, so too does the percent of students with a diagnosed disability, except for schools with the greatest minority population. Only two institutions, however, are included in this category.

Table 3.1: Proportion of Students with Diagnosed Disability by Minority Student Population

% of School's Population Minority (Number of Schools in Category)	Mean % of School's Population with Diagnosed Disability
Minority population < 25% (N=78)	8.2%
Minority population 25-50% (N=17)	11.77%
Minority population 51-75% (N=8)	19.0%
Minority population <75% (N=2)	5.0%

Overall, 61 percent of principals reported that their schools require information about a prospective student's disability during the application process. Schools in the Great Lakes and Plains states and rural schools were significantly less likely to require information from their applicants than schools in the other regions or urban, inner city, or suburban schools. For example, 35 percent of Plains and 55 percent of Great Lakes schools required information about a student's disability, compared to 71-90 percent of schools in the other regions, and 100 percent of inner city schools reported having this requirement compared with 34 percent of rural schools.

Principals were asked to indicate the number of current students in their schools who have been diagnosed with one of 12 possible disabilities. Table 3.2 provides the mean percent by disability type *among those who have been diagnosed with a disability*. For example, of those who have a disability, the three most common types were a specific learning disability, such as dyslexia, other health impairment, such as ADHD, and speech or language impairments. There is a potential for comorbidity (students having several diagnoses), so percentages will not total 100 percent.

Table 3.2: Proportion of Students with Disabilities with Each Disability Type

Disability Type	Number Responding	Mean	Median
Specific learning disability (e.g., dyslexia)	101	33.8%	30.7%
Other health impairment (e.g., ADHD)	95	35.9%	33.3%
Autism spectrum disorder	89	14.0%	8.0%
Emotional disturbance (e.g., anxiety, OCD)	74	7.5%	3.1%
Speech or language impairment	95	34.3%	25.9%
Visual impairment, including blindness	70	1.3%	0%
Deafness	67	<0.5%	0%
Hearing impairment	76	5.4%	0%
Deaf-Blindness	65	<.5%	0%
Orthopedic impairment (e.g., cerebral palsy)	72	1.8%	0%
Intellectual disability (e.g., Down syndrome)	72	2.2%	0%
Traumatic brain injury	69	<.5%	0%

Chapter 4

Policies, Procedures and Protocols

Written Policies

Among superintendents, three-quarters reported that there are written policies in the diocesan handbook about the provision of services for students with disabilities, but just over one-third have a separate handbook, outlining common systems of support for meeting the needs of students with disabilities in diocesan schools. Slightly less than one-half of the respondent superintendents have a designated person in the diocesan office who oversees the delivery of services to students with disabilities and who oversees the government programs related to services for students with disabilities.

Just over one-third of principals reported that they have written policies for including students with disabilities into the school. Regarding referrals, 64 percent of principals reported that their schools have a written policy to refer students with a suspected disability for further testing. Roughly one-half require Tier I and II intervention in a Response to Intervention model (RtI) before a student is referred for a comprehensive evaluation. Principals were asked who initiates referrals for disability testing. Response options included parents, classroom teachers, special needs teachers, social services and other. In total, two-thirds were able to provide a full accounting of their referrals from one of the five sources. Classroom teachers were the most endorsed. Principals reported that 66 percent of referrals came from their classroom teachers. Other referrals, on average, came from: parents (32 percent), special needs teachers (18 percent), social services (1 percent) and other (6 percent). Some endorsed figures greater than 100 percent due to students being referred by multiple parties.

Admission Procedures

Principals were asked if they would admit students with certain known disabilities (see Figures 4.1-4.14). Principals reported they were most likely to admit students with disabilities similar to those of their current disabled student populations (i.e. specific learning disability, other health impairment or a speech or language impairment). The majority reported that they would consider admitting students with any of the disabilities, apart from deaf-blindness, depending on the severity of the disability. Schools seemed to feel least equipped to work with students with sensory disabilities, including hearing and vision loss, as well as students with intellectual disabilities or traumatic brain injuries.

Figure 4.1: Admission Decisions by Disability Category: Multiple Disabilities

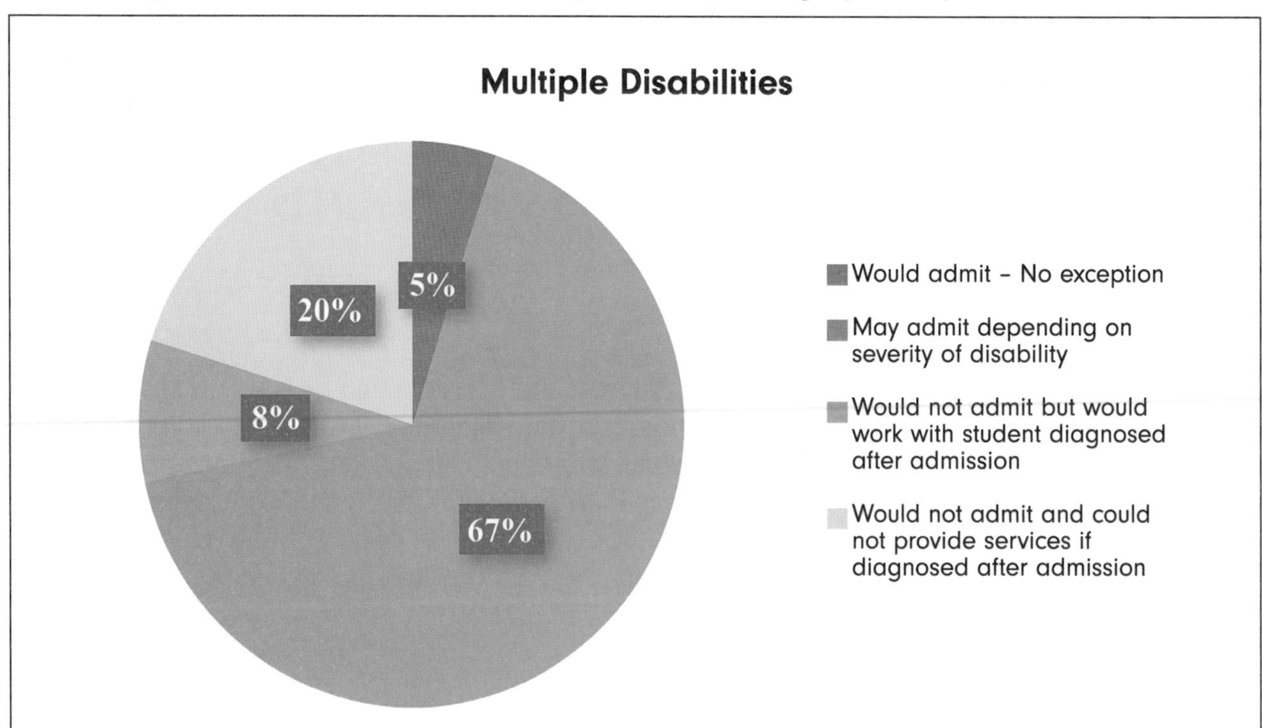

Figure 4.2: Admission Decisions by Disability Category: Traumatic Brain Injury

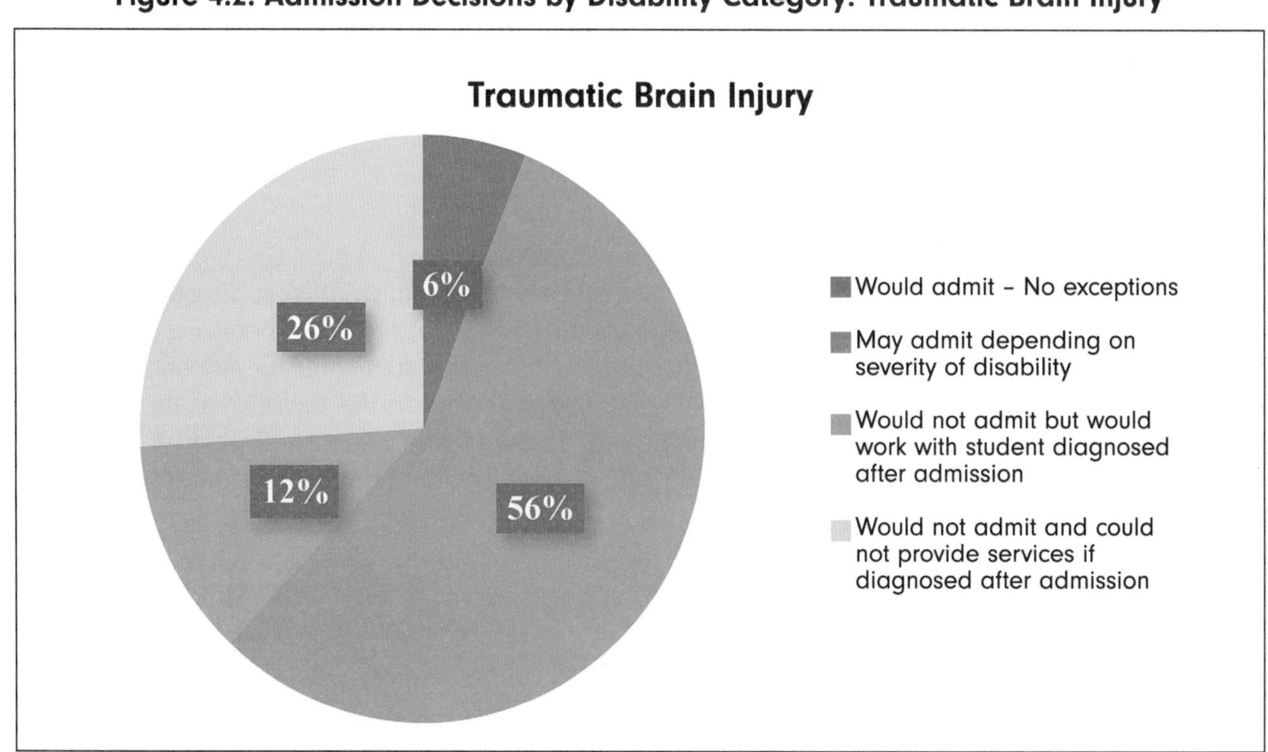

Figure 4.3: Admission Decisions by Disability Category: Intellectual Disability

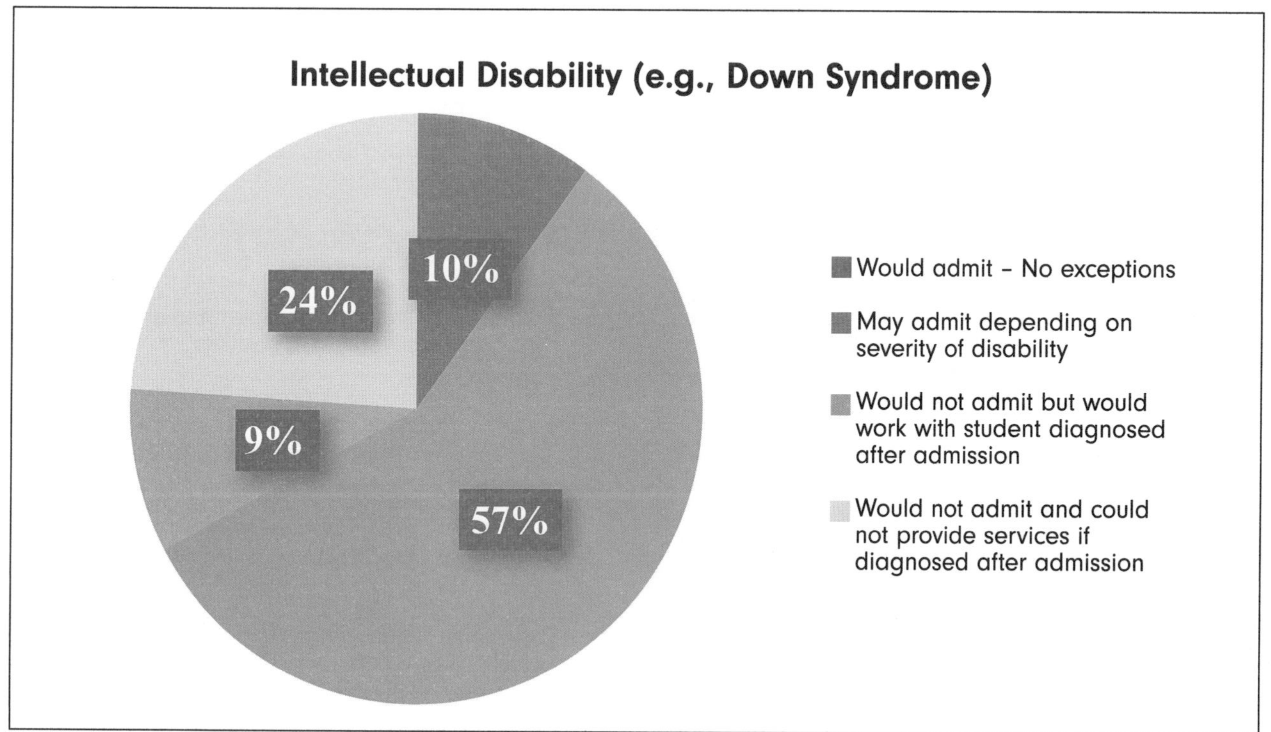

Figure 4.4: Admission Decisions by Disability Category: Orthopedic Impairment

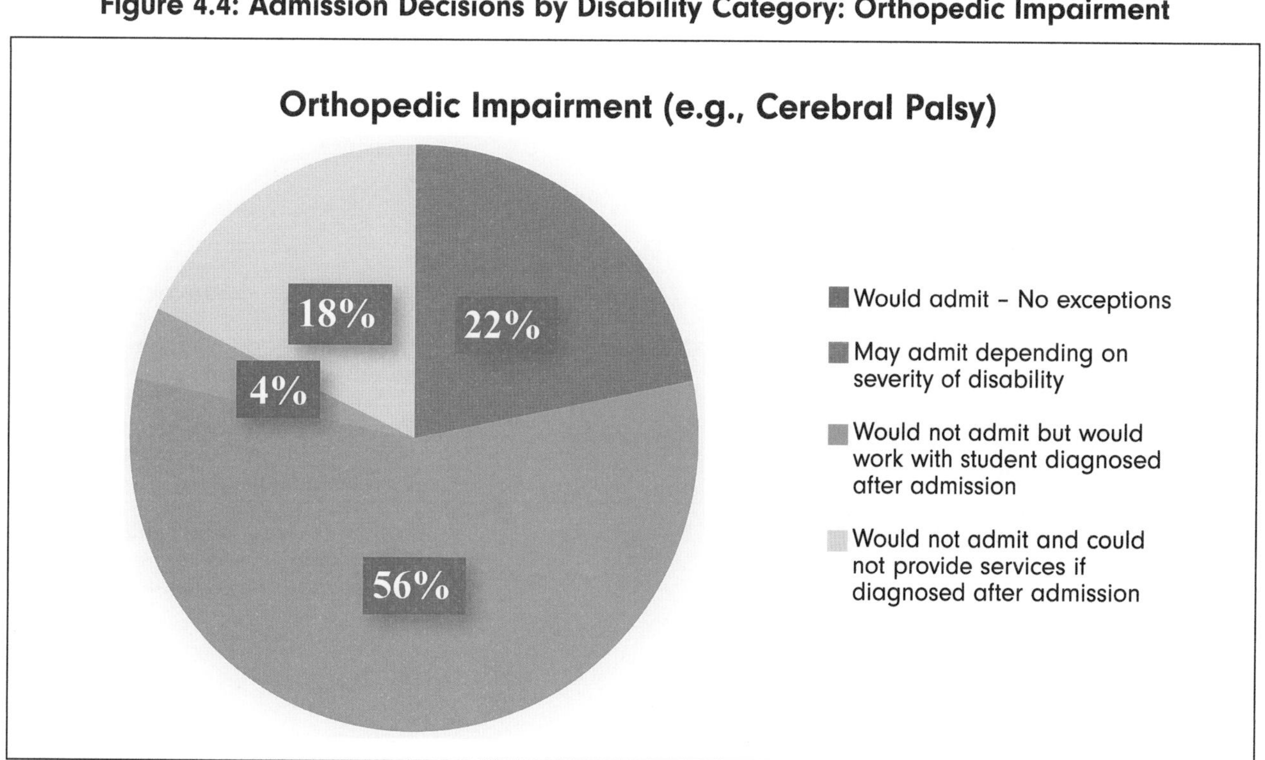

Figure 4.5: Admission Decisions by Disability Category: Deaf-Blindness

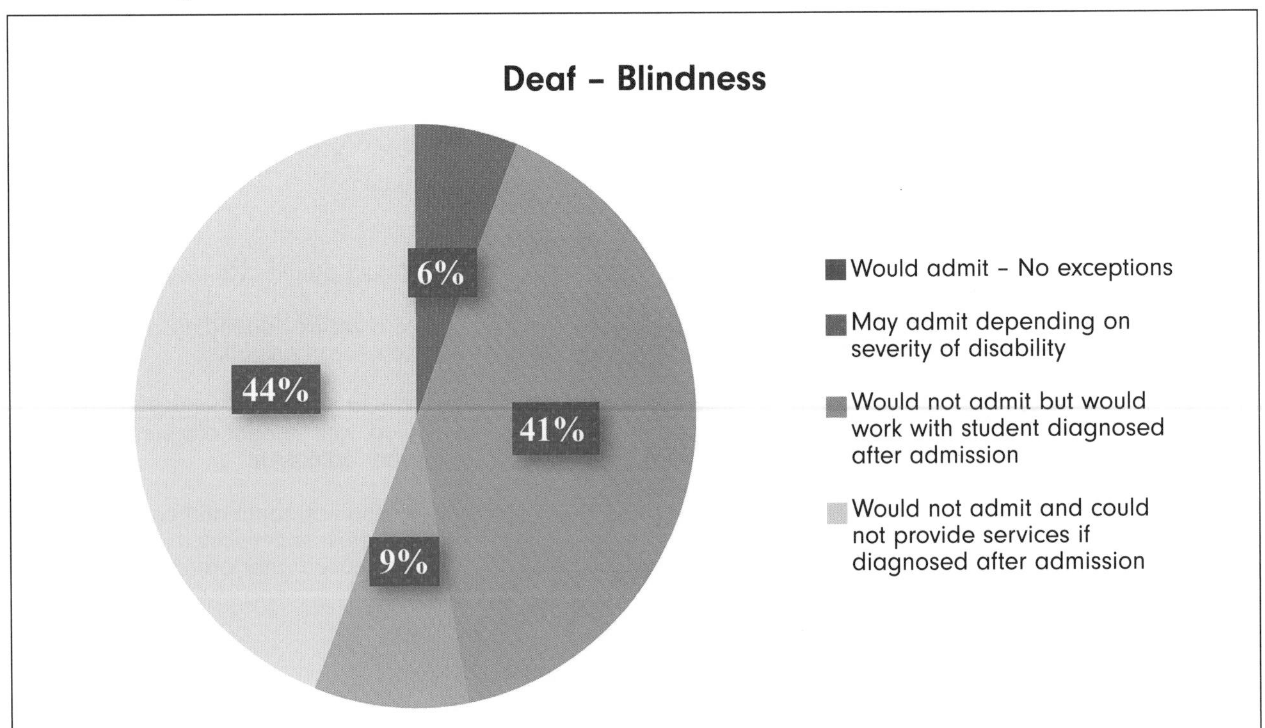

Figure 4.6: Admission Decisions by Disability Category: Hearing Impairment

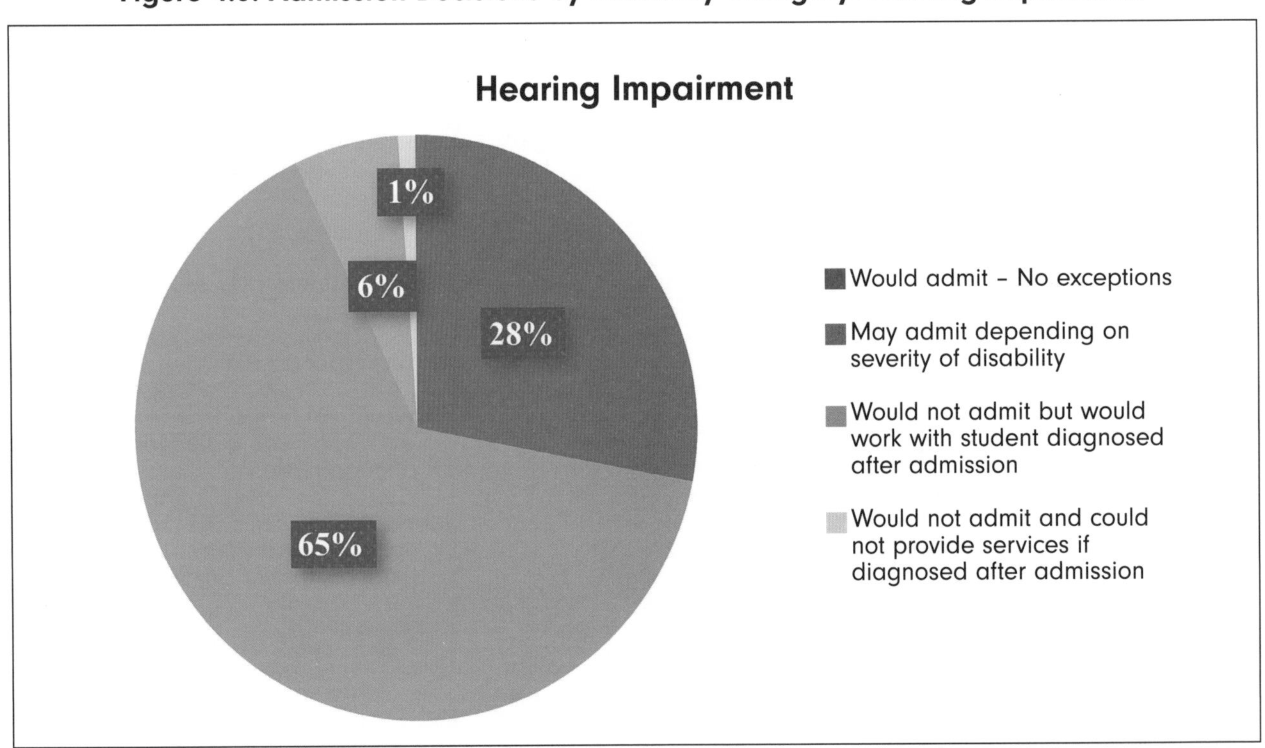

Figure 4.7: Admission Decisions by Disability Category: Deafness

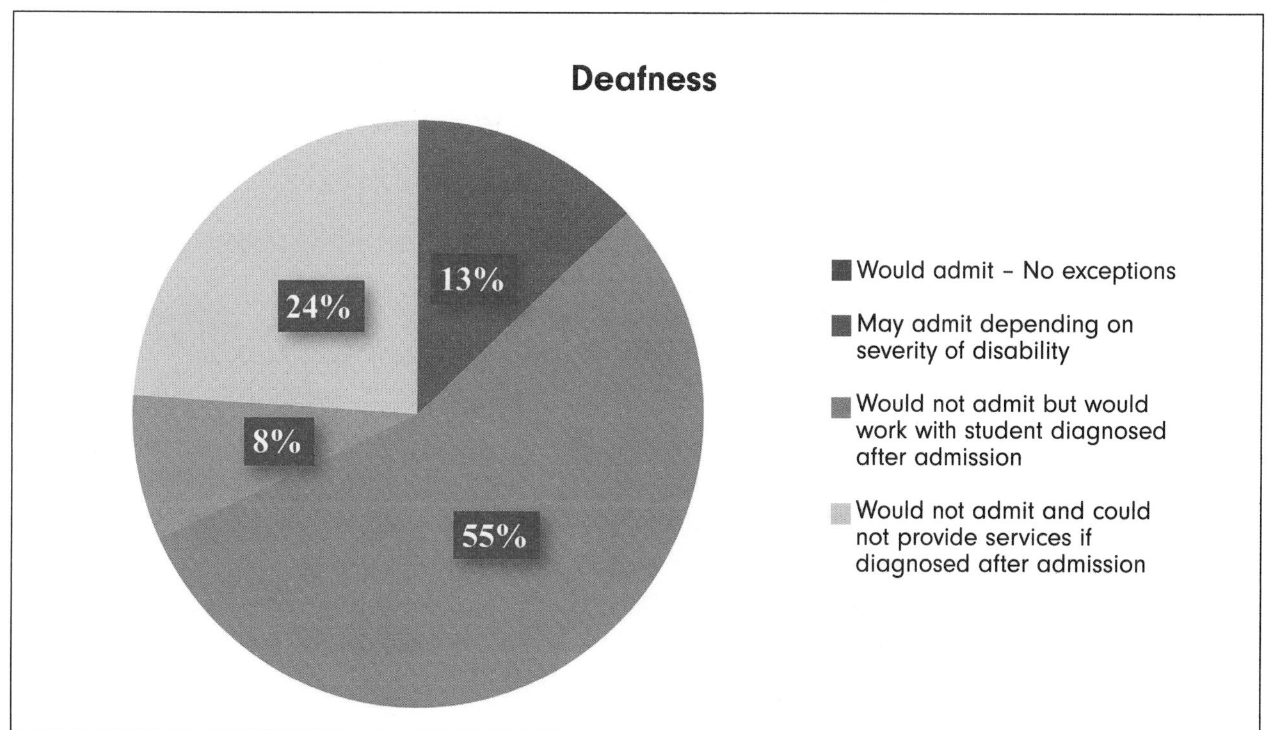

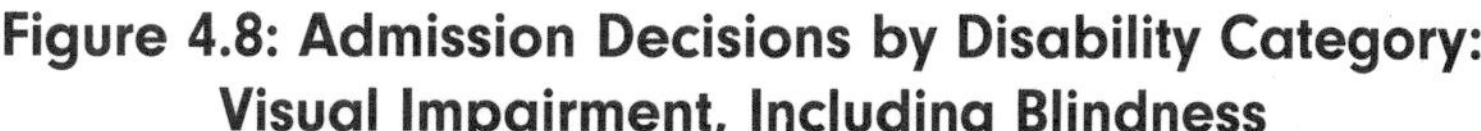

Figure 4.8: Admission Decisions by Disability Category: Visual Impairment, Including Blindness

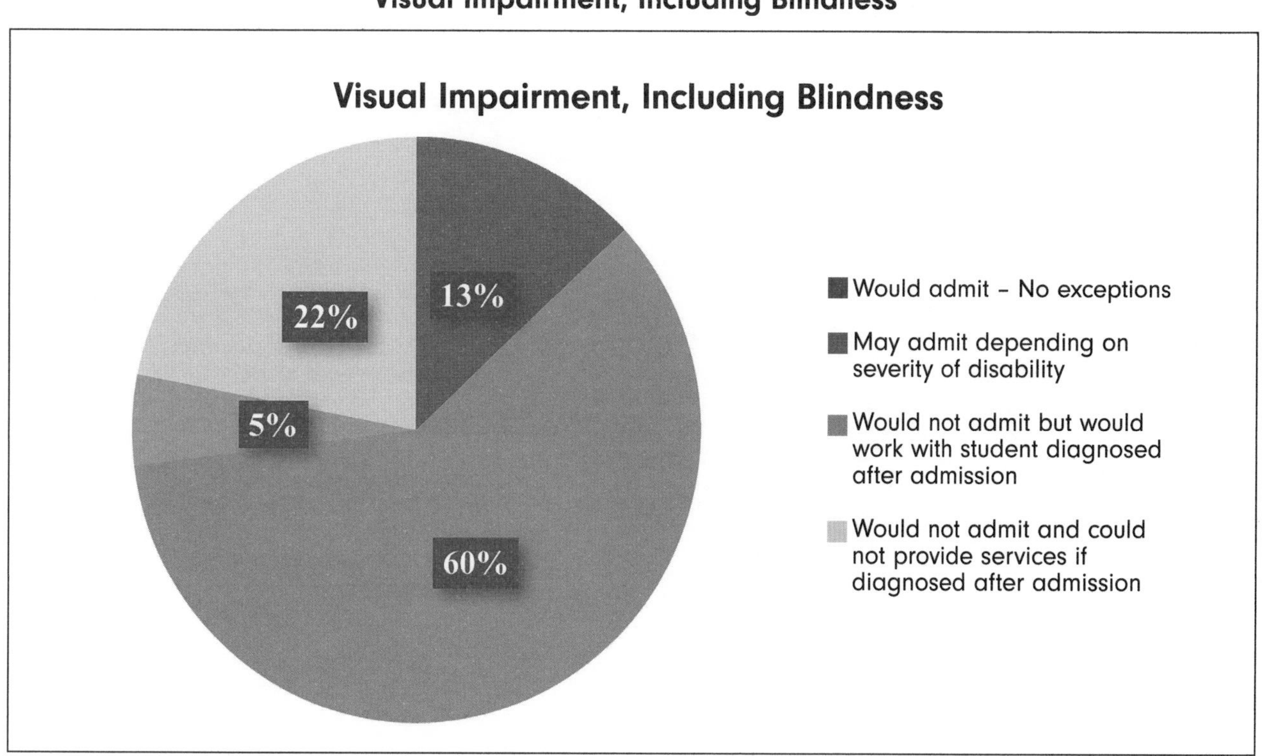

Figure 4.9: Admission Decisions by Disability Category: Speech or Language Impairment

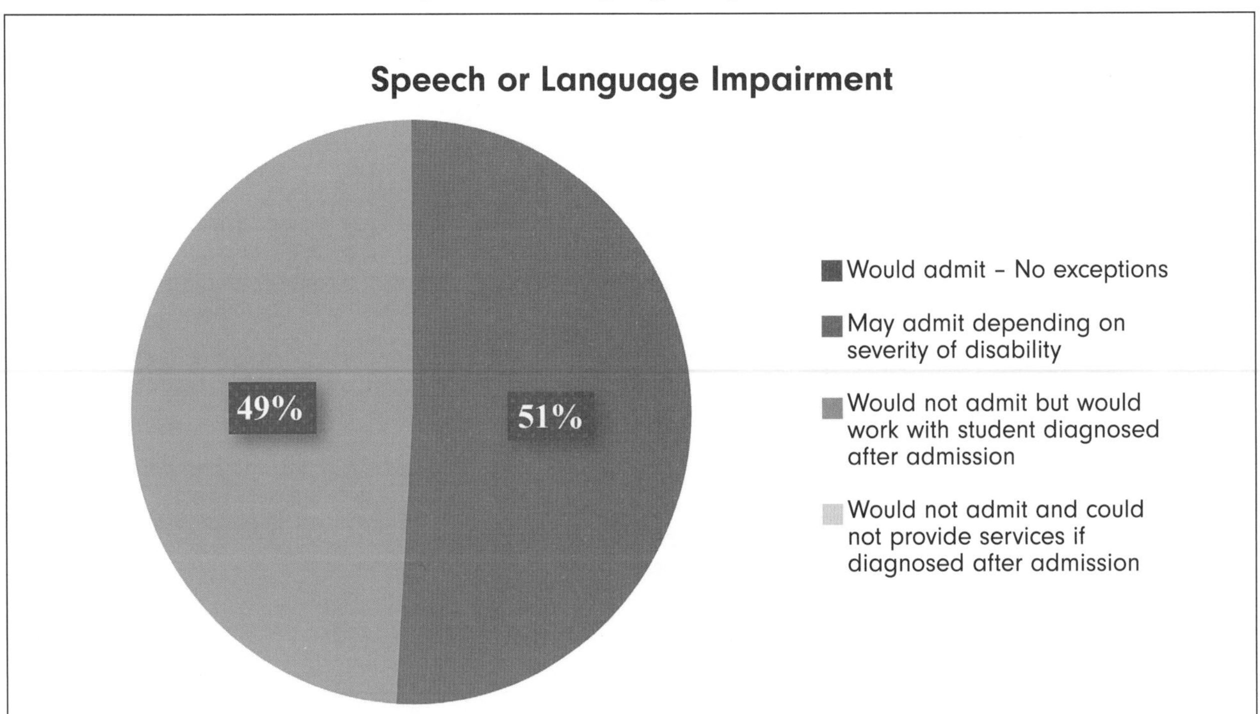

Figure 4.10: Admission Decisions by Disability Category: Emotional Disturbance

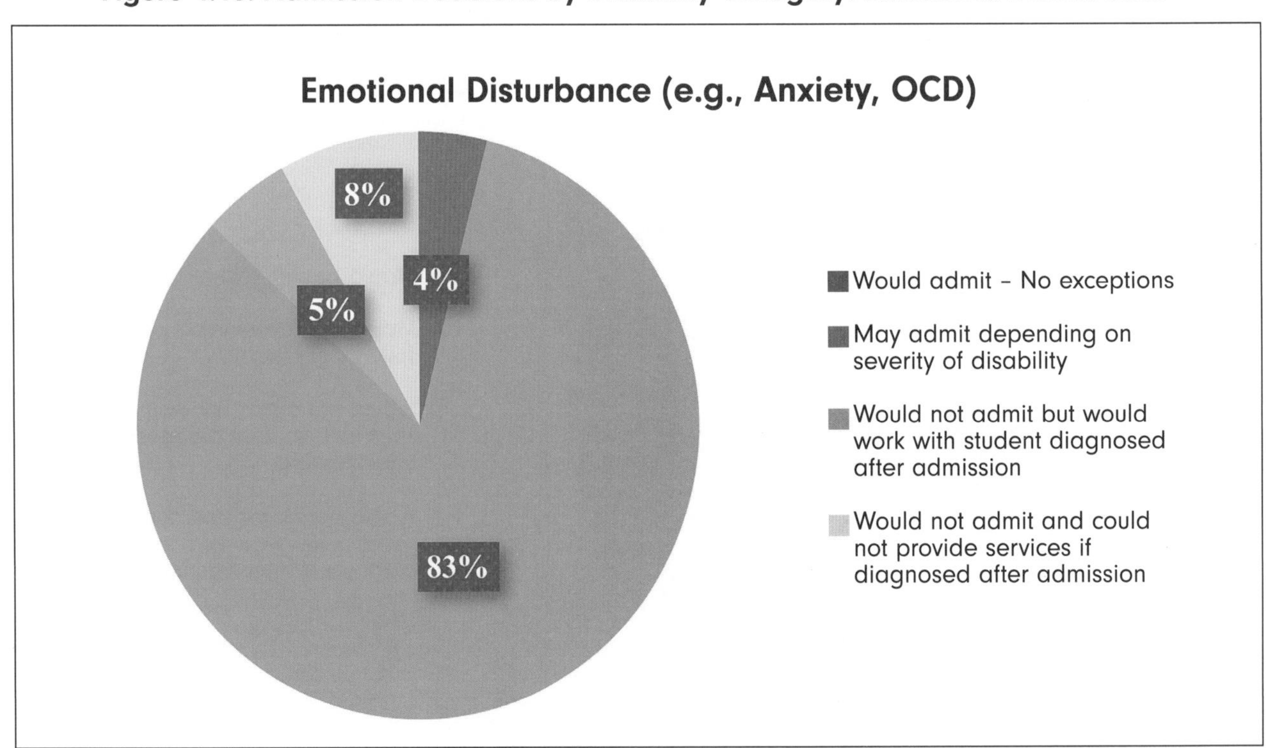

Figure 4.11: Admission Decisions by Disability Category: Autism Spectrum Disorder

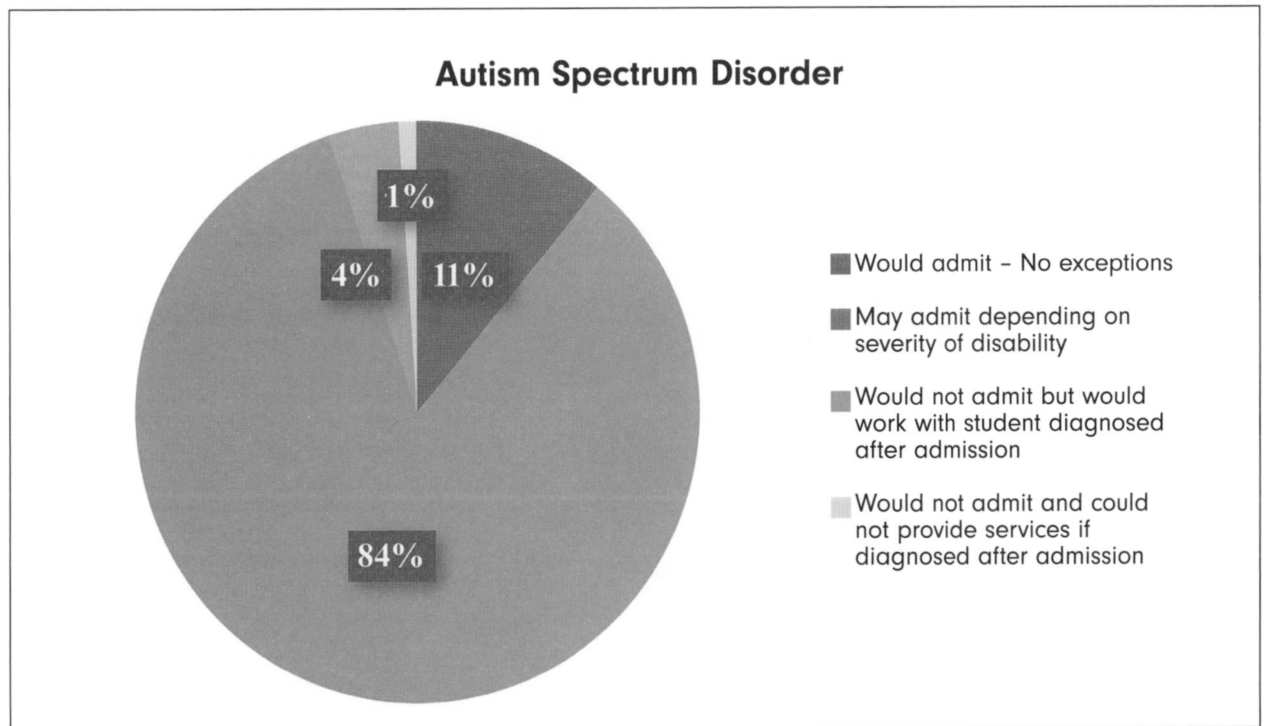

Figure 4.12: Admission Decisions by Disability Category: Other Health Impairment

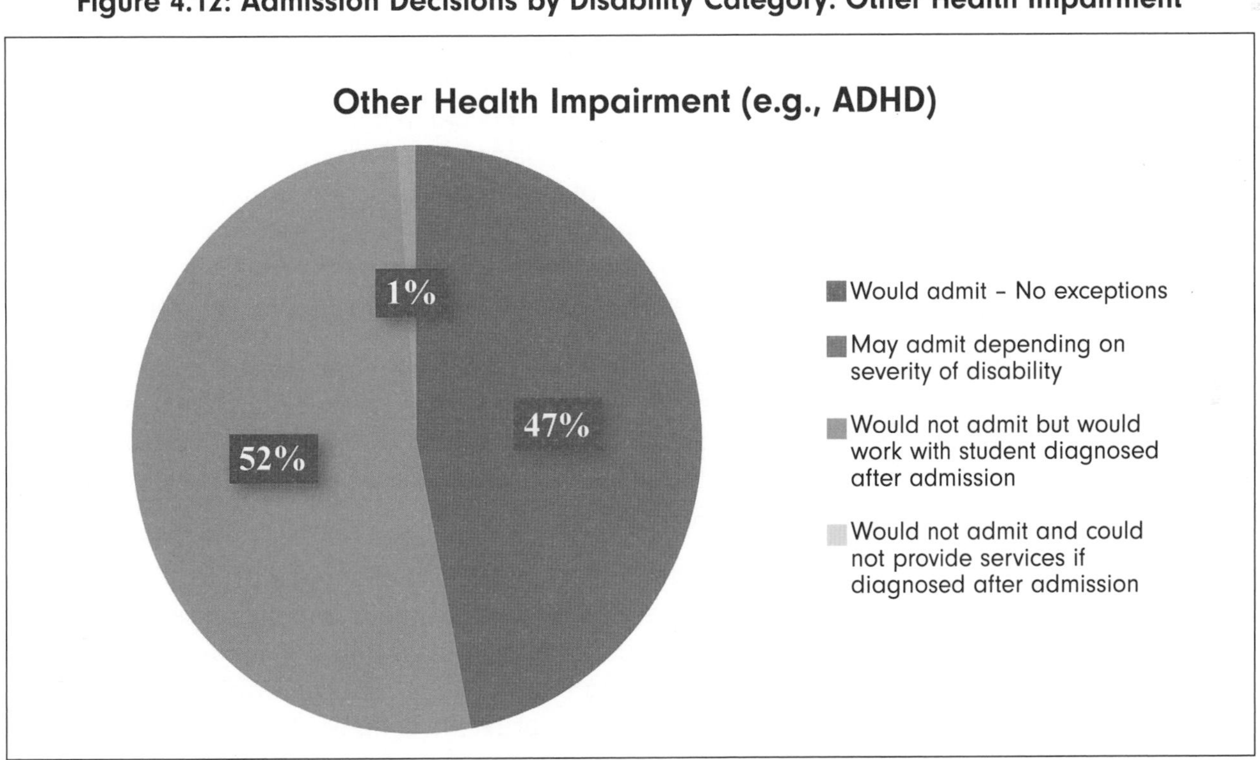

Figure 4.13: Admission Decisions by Disability Category: Specific Learning Disability

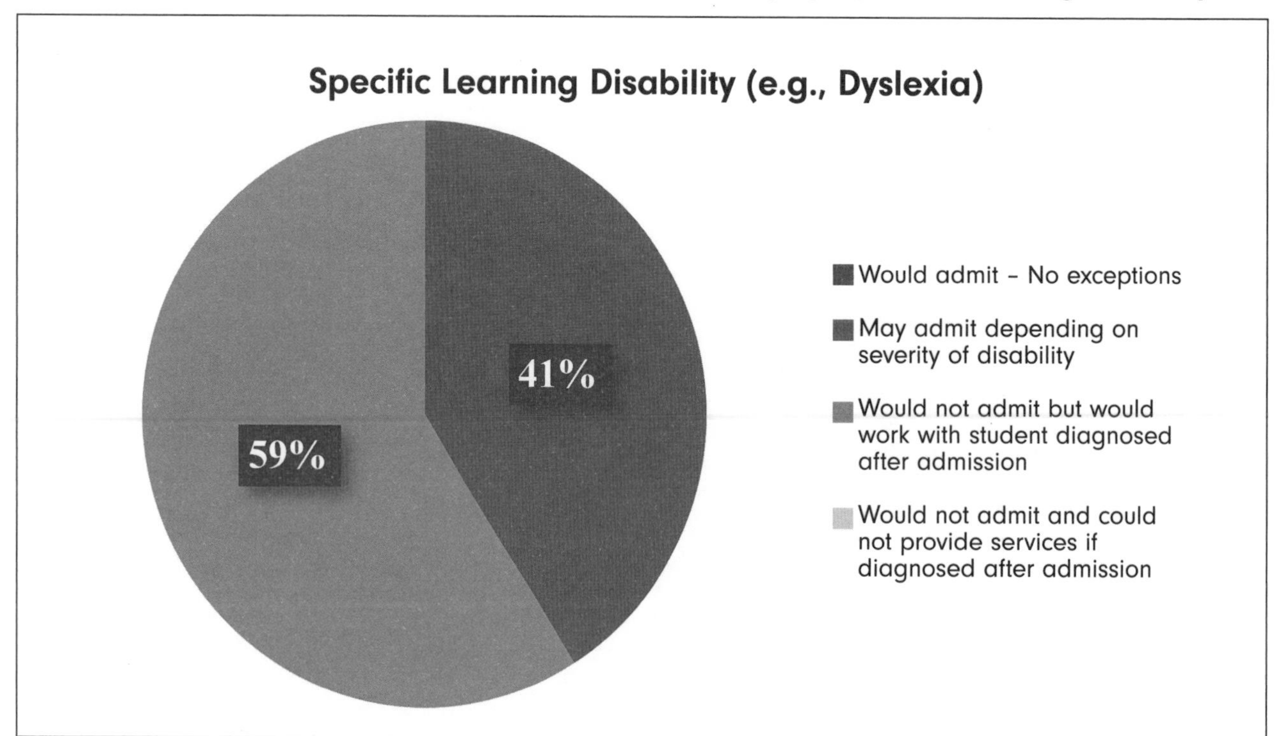

Principals were asked to provide additional comments regarding the process for considering students for admission with various disabilities, including mobility, sensory, and cognitive. Common themes throughout included the need to evaluate admission on a case-by-case basis. The need for the parents to be a part of the process was heavily supported by the respondent principals. Many mentioned the importance of evaluating the specific needs of the students and the severity of the disabilities to determine if they could be successful at their schools. As one principal wrote, *"Administration meets with family to become familiar with the family and to understand the needs of the student. If reasonable accommodations can be made, an agreement is written up and monitored throughout the year."* Knowing the child's needs would be met was of paramount importance. One principal wrote, *"We believe it is a moral imperative to work with any family who desires a Catholic education. Frank discussions are held to clarify the school's willingness and ability to meet the needs of the learner. If the parents and principal are able to craft a shared vision, an educational partnership begins."*

Regarding mobility disabilities, several schools mentioned that it would be difficult to impossible to accommodate a student with a mobility disability because their schools are not compliant with the Americans with Disabilities Act (ADA). When considering students with sensory disabilities, financial considerations were mentioned by some, including any additional professional development for teachers and whether the family would be able to contribute.

One principal mentioned that they work with a local public school to help provide services, including a sign language interpreter who works with both the Catholic and public school. Finally, for students with cognitive disabilities, the process for considering admission focuses a great deal on evaluating individual cases, including reviewing the individual education plans if they have them, evaluation of testing, and consultations with their previous schools. Most schools indicated an ability to work with students with cognitive disabilities, although for some, it did depend on the severity and the extent of accommodations that would be needed.

This emphasis on individual needs assessment is consistent with the principals' own perceptions of how accessible their schools are. Over one-half consider their schools "somewhat accessible" to students with sensory or cognitive disabilities, while responses to mobility accessibility are fairly mixed (see Figure 4.14).

Figure 4.14: Principals' Perceived Accessibility of School by Disability Type

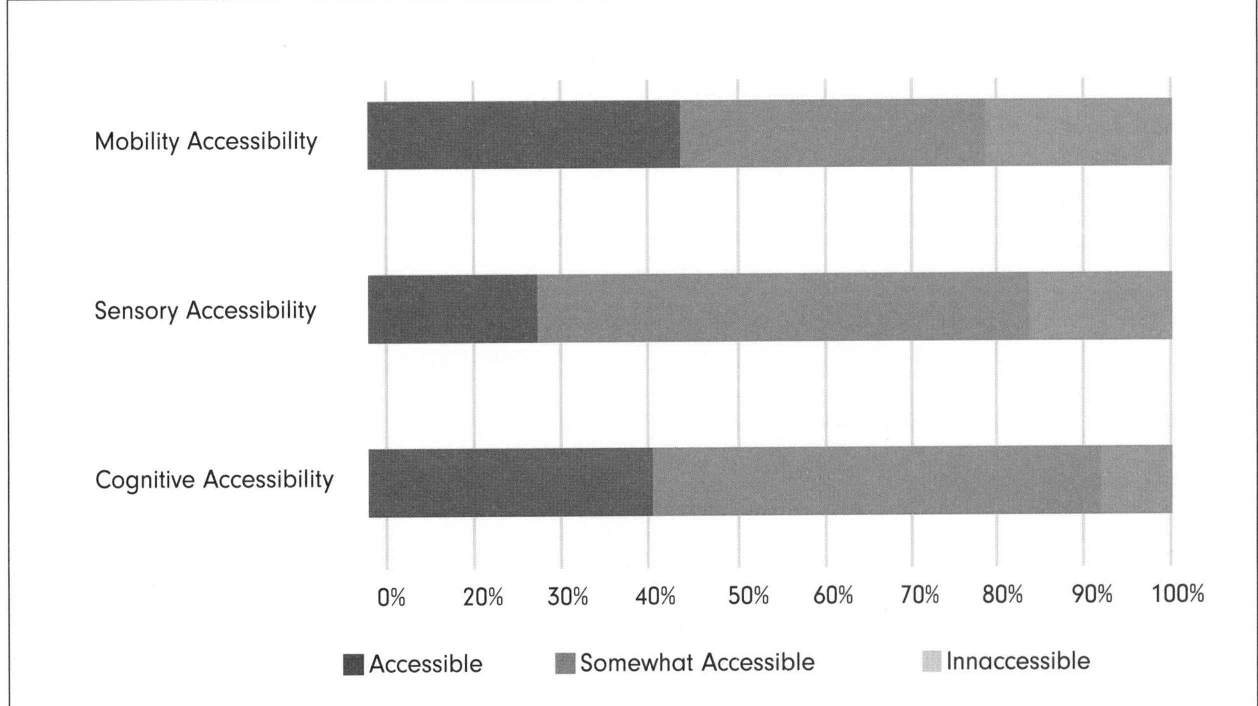

Diagnostic and Disability Determination Process

On average, principals report that 45 percent of their students were diagnosed *after* enrollment in their institutions. There was no significant difference in the percent of students diagnosed after enrollment when comparing schools that do and do not require information about a student's potential disabilities during the application process.

Schools use a combination of several other means to help identify if a student has a suspected disability. Among the most common are classroom performance and observations and psychological evaluations (see Figure 4.15). Discipline records and universal screenings are used comparatively less frequently. There was no difference in schools' characteristics that use these two methods compared with those that do not.

Figure 4.15: Percent Reporting Use of Each of the Following Methods to Diagnose Disabilities as Reported by Principals

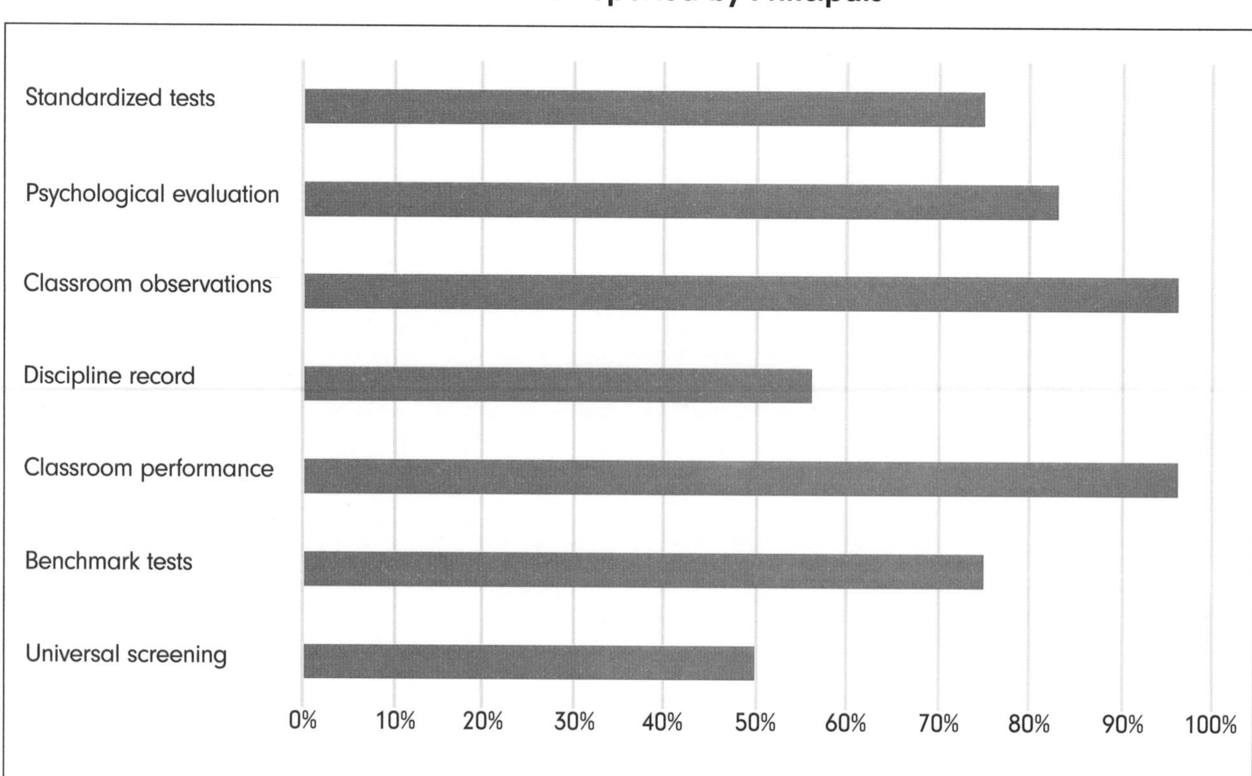

Overall, 73 percent of principals indicated that they have students they suspect have a disability who have not yet been diagnosed. Nearly every principal of an urban school reported having this concern (93 percent), followed by suburban principals (72 percent), and rural principals (58 percent). The most common reason principals attribute to this is the resistance of parents to pursue a diagnosis (see Figure 4.16), with 64 percent of the principals endorsing either "Strongly Agree" or "Agree." In terms of the evaluation process, just over one-quarter of principals reported that they at least *somewhat agree* that the Catholic school process is too cumbersome, compared with nearly two-thirds who believe the public school process is too cumbersome (see Figure 4.17 and Figure 4.18).

Figure 4.16: Percent of Principals Reporting Agreement that Parents are Resistant to the Evaluation Process

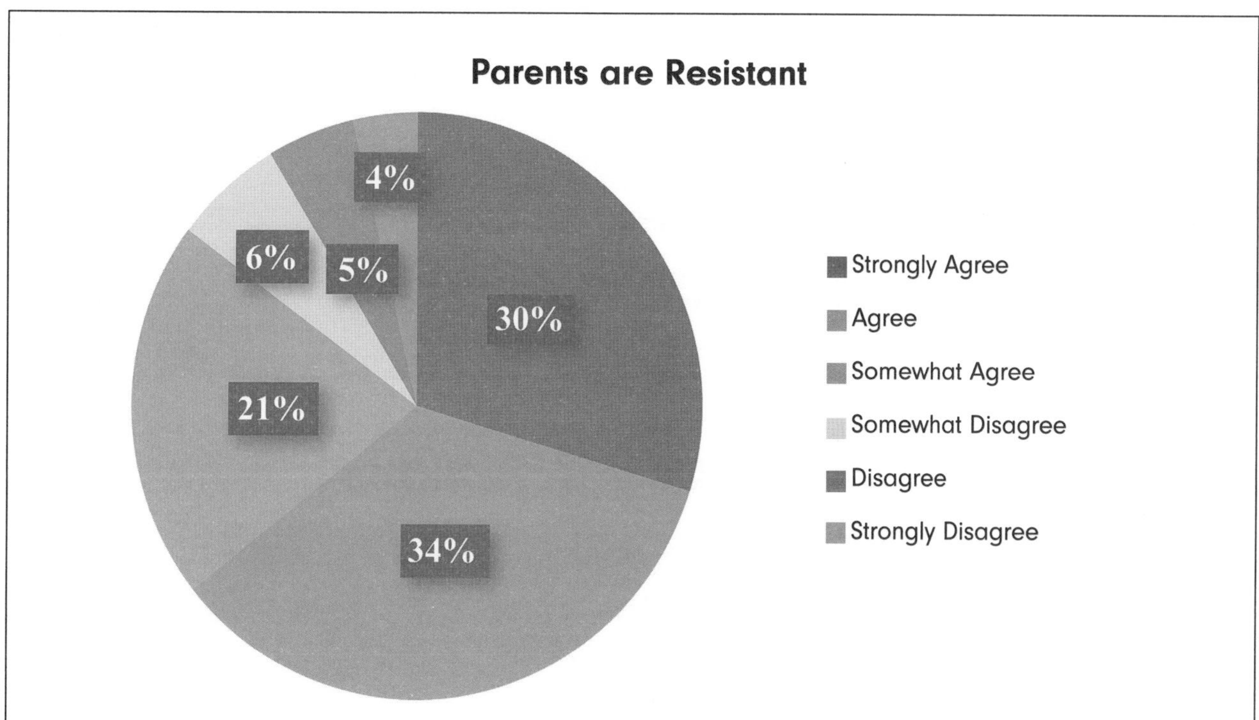

Figure 4.17: Percentage of Principals Reporting that the Public School Process is too Cumbersome.

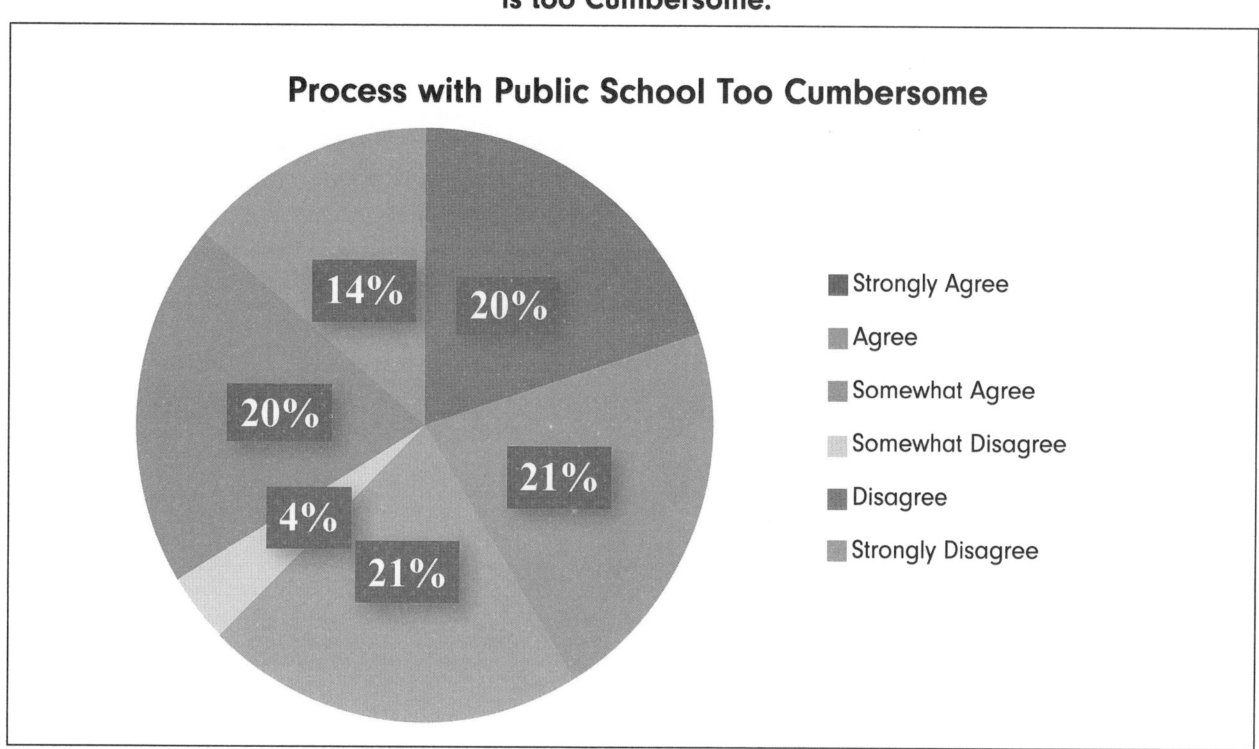

Figure 4.18: Percentage of Principals Reporting that the Catholic School Process is too Cumbersome.

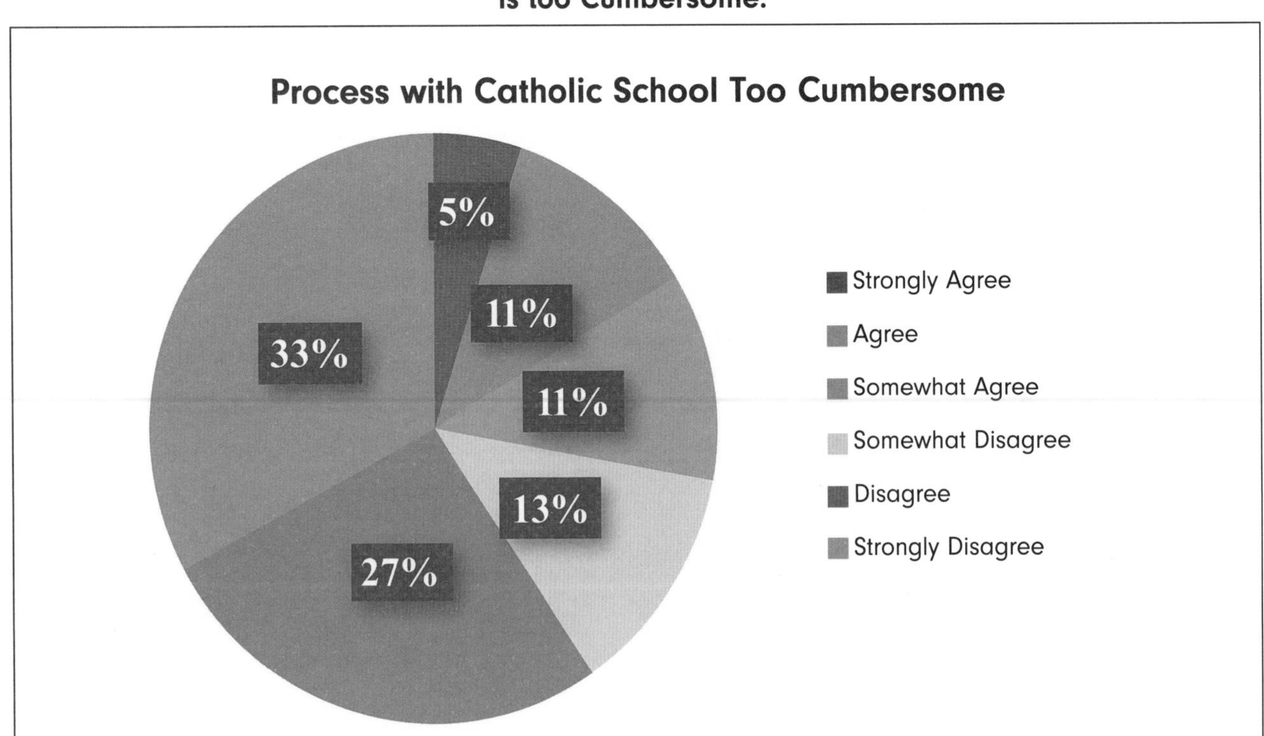

Principals were asked who initiated referrals for disability testing. Response options included parents, classroom teachers, special needs teachers, social service and other. In total, two-thirds were able to provide a full accounting of their referrals from one of the five sources. Classroom teachers were the most endorsed. Principals reported that 66 percent of referrals came from their classroom teachers. Other referrals, on average, came from: parents (32 percent), special needs teachers (18 percent), social service (1 percent) and other (6 percent). Some endorsed figures greater than 100 percent due to students being referred by multiple parties.

Students are nearly 3.5 times as likely to be sent to a public school evaluator as opposed to a private evaluator if they are suspected of having a disability. When asked, however, what percent then are found to have a disability when reviewed by the different evaluators, there was no difference by statistical standards between public school and private evaluators. Roughly three-fourths of students referred to either are found to have a disability.

Chapter 5

Provision of Services

Types of Services Offered

Of the principals who were surveyed, over one-half offer the following support services: inclusion, resource support, counseling, speech and language services, and paraprofessionals. A lack of personnel is the most common reason for not offering a service. In addition to the services delineated in the survey, principals were offered the opportunity to list other interventions that did not appear on the list. The results by service area can be found in Figures 5.1 -5.10. The principals most frequently cited some type of academic intervention – tutoring, homework club, or afterschool math help, for example. When asked what one service they do not currently offer but would like to offer, occupational and physical therapy and counseling / psychological services were the most frequently mentioned. Lack of funding was the most common cause for not offering these services.

Figure 5.1: Principals Who Report Offering Inclusion

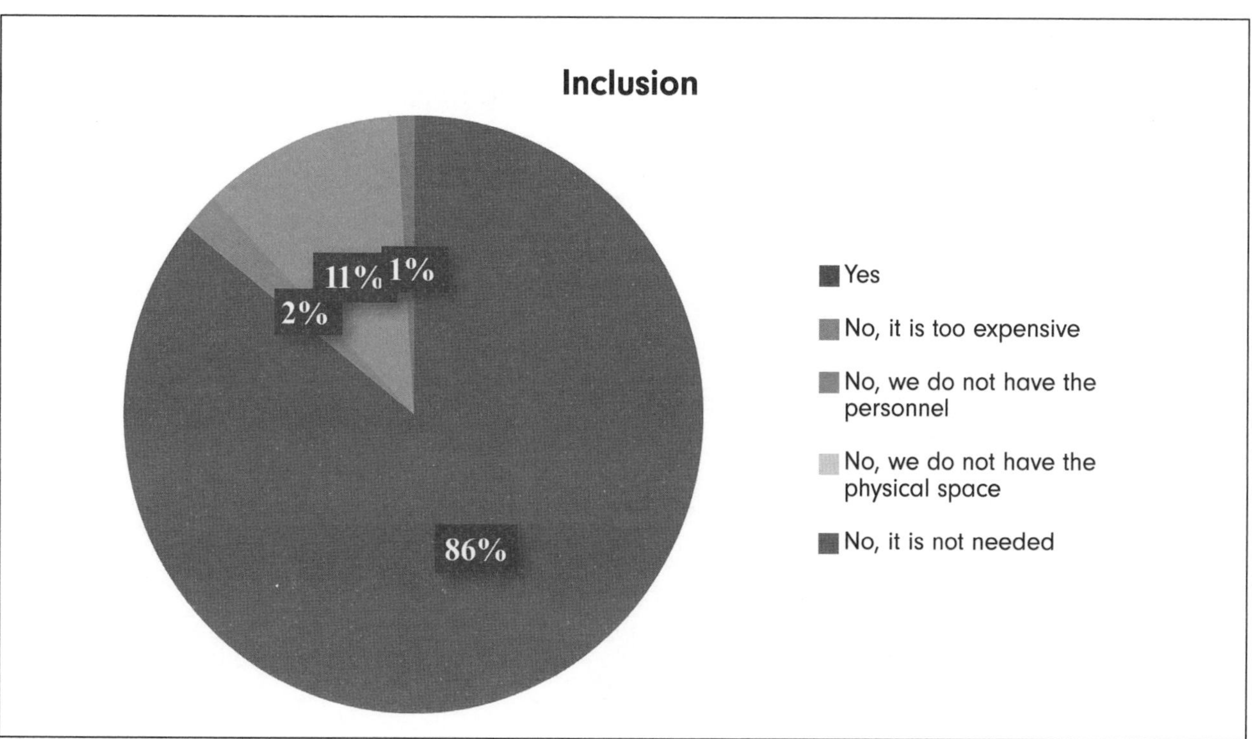

Figure 5.2: Principals Who Report Offering Resource Support

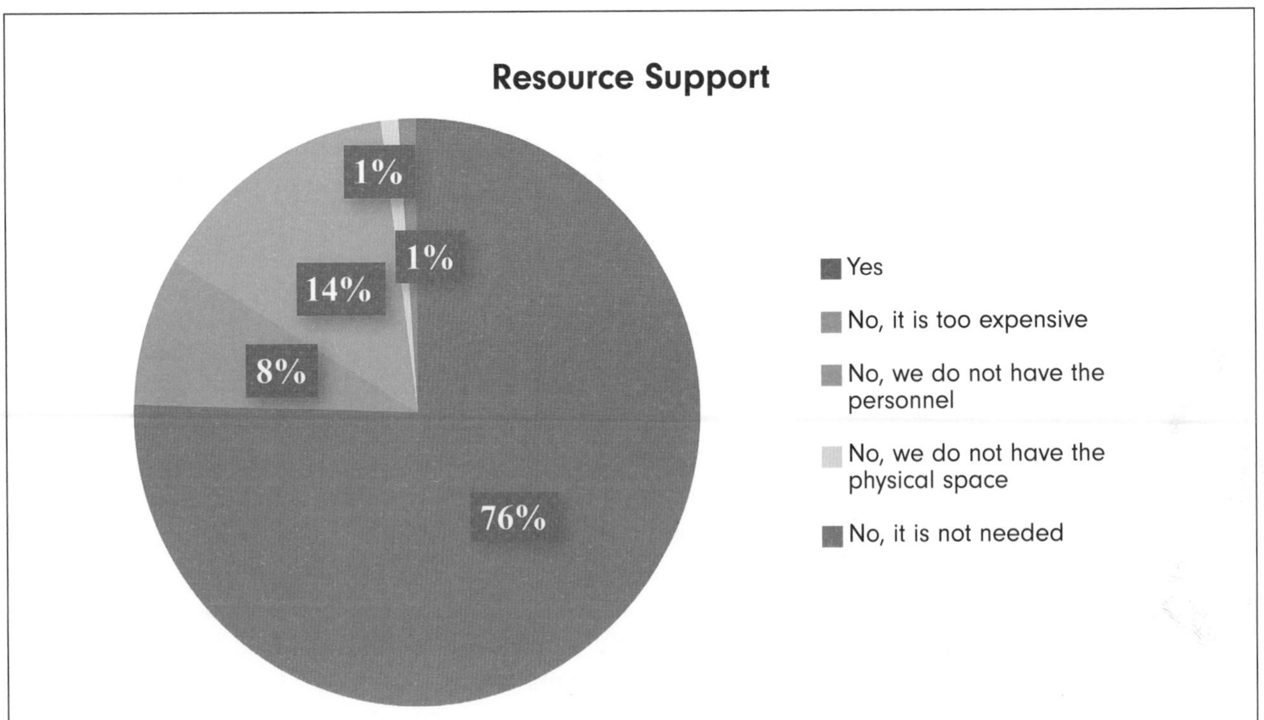

Figure 5.3: Principals Who Report Offering Counseling Support

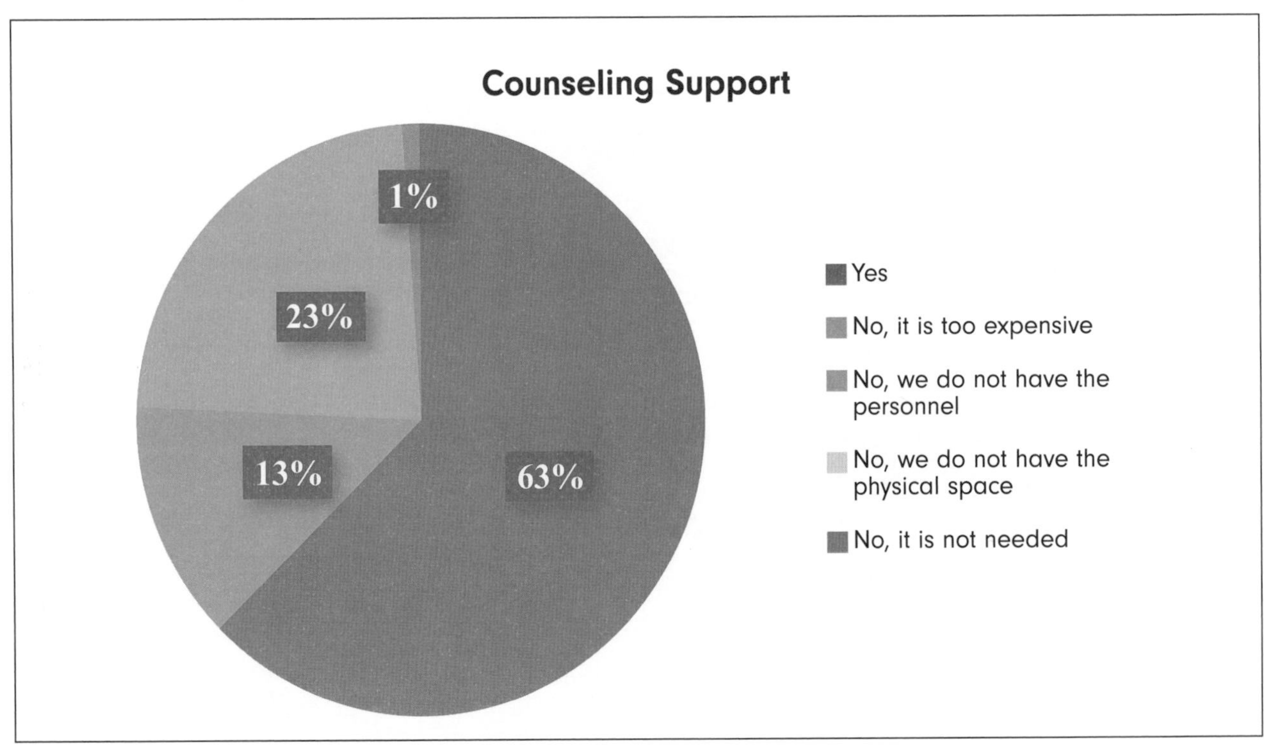

Figure 5.4: Principals Who Report Offering Speech and Language Support

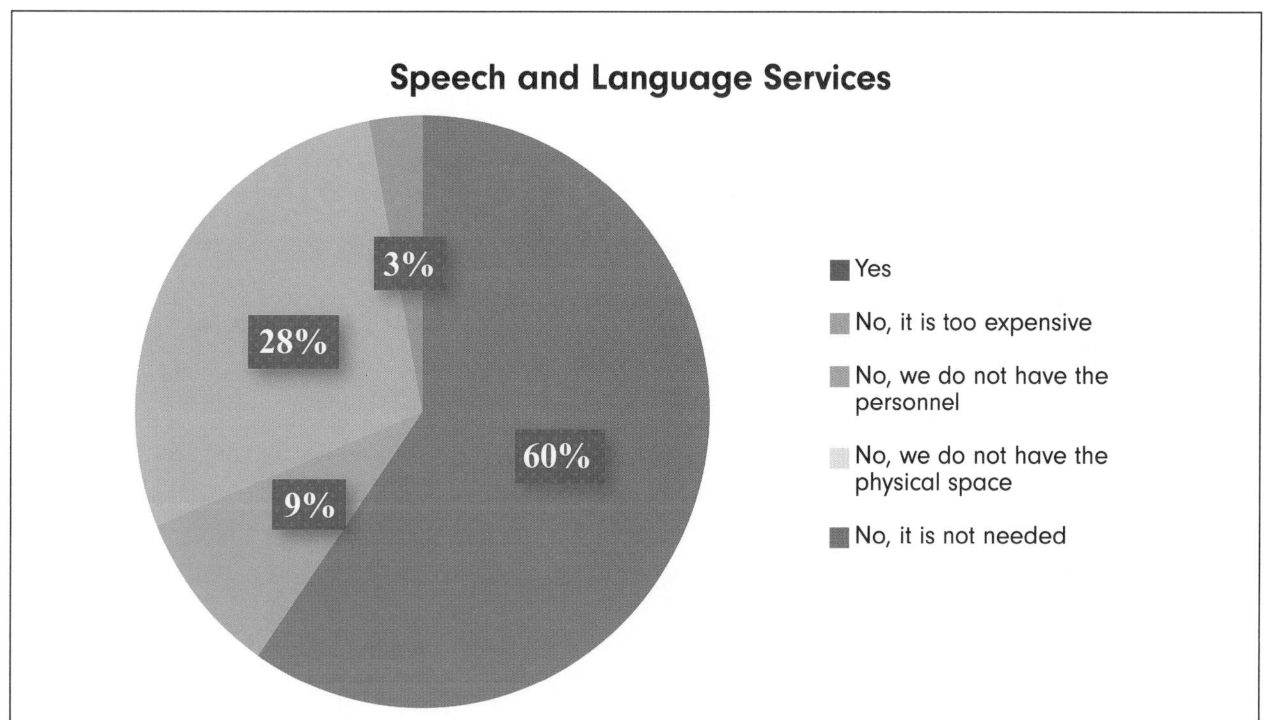

Figure 5.5: Principals Who Report Using Paraprofessionals

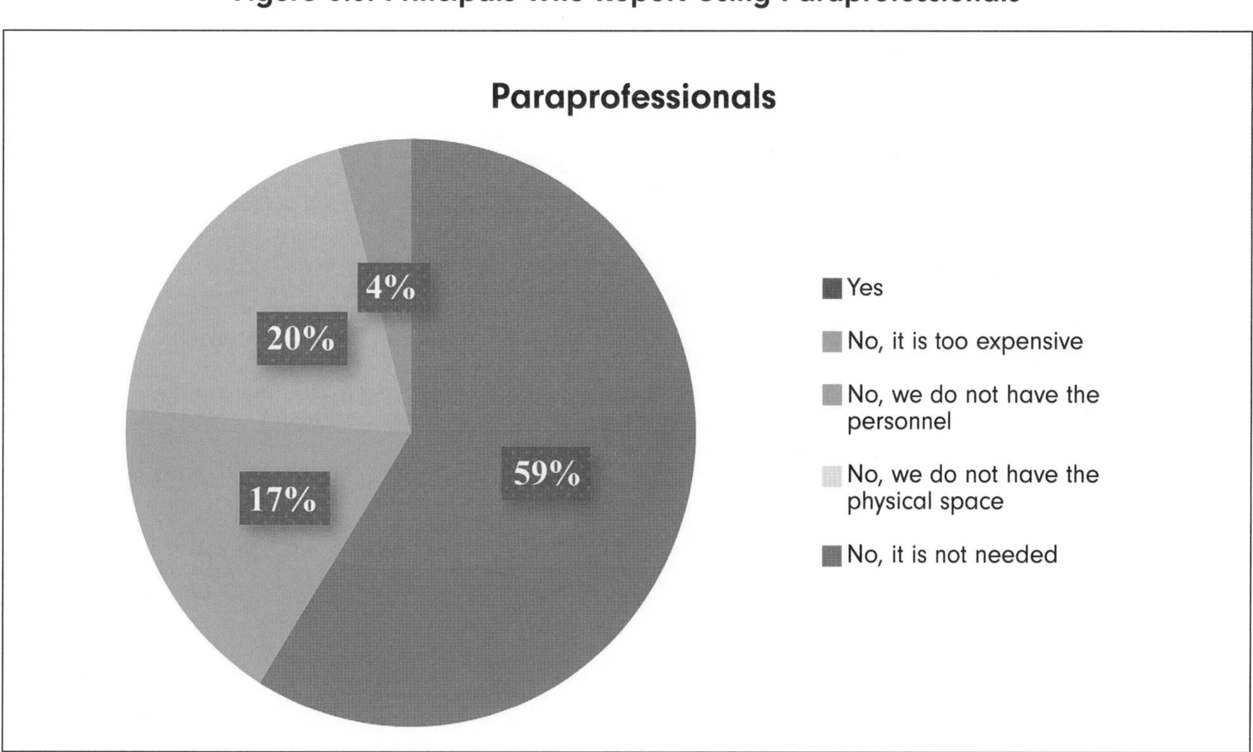

Figure 5.6: Principals Who Report Offering Nursing Services

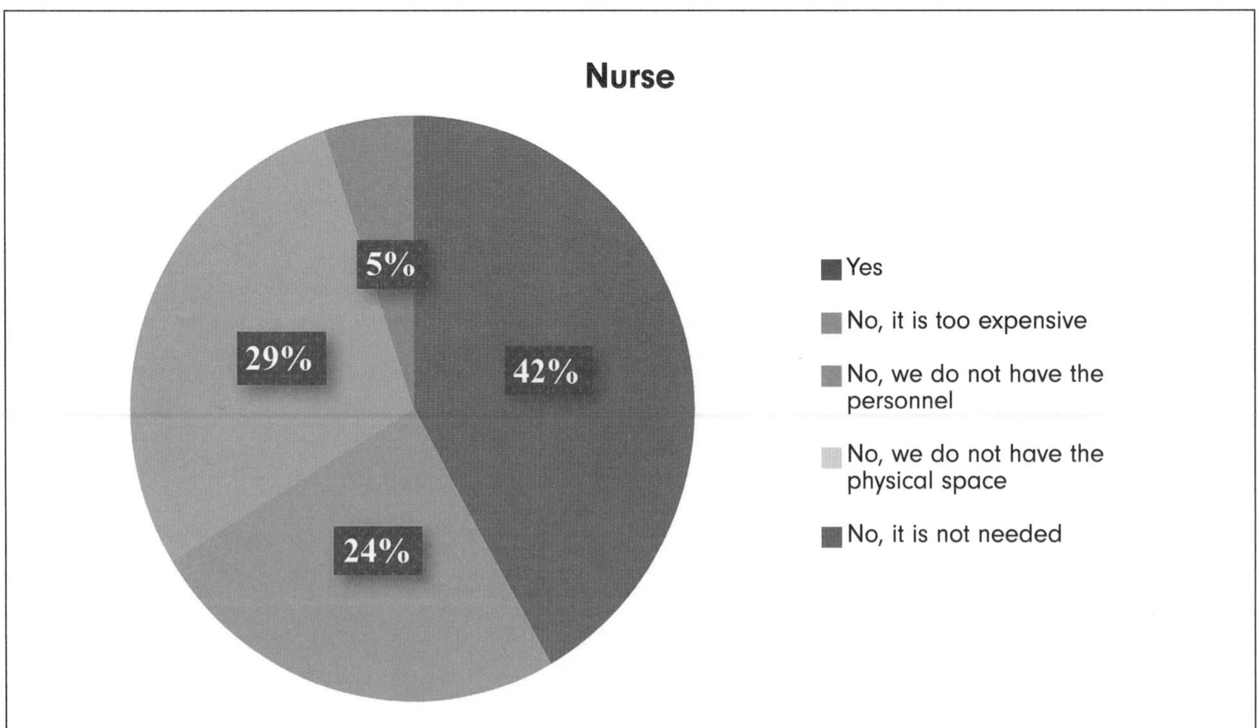

Figure 5.7: Principals Who Report Utilizing Co-Teaching

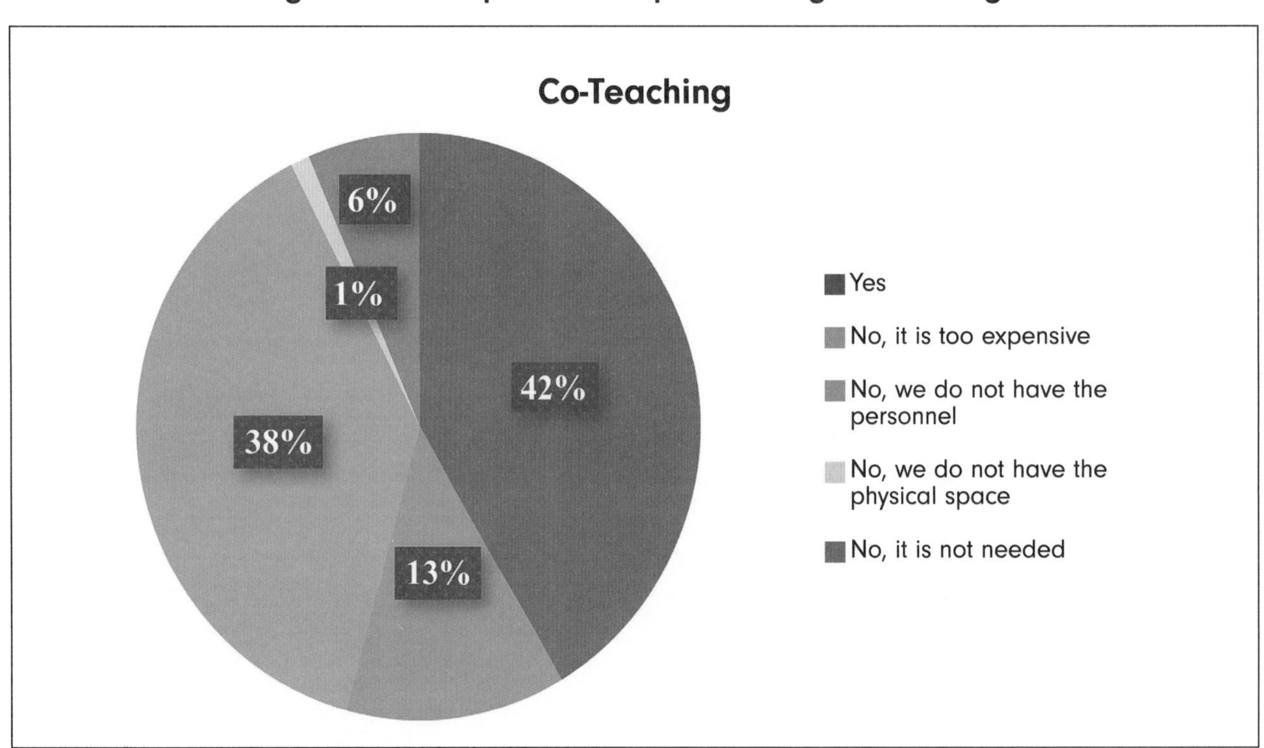

Figure 5.8: Principals Who Report Offering Occupational Therapy

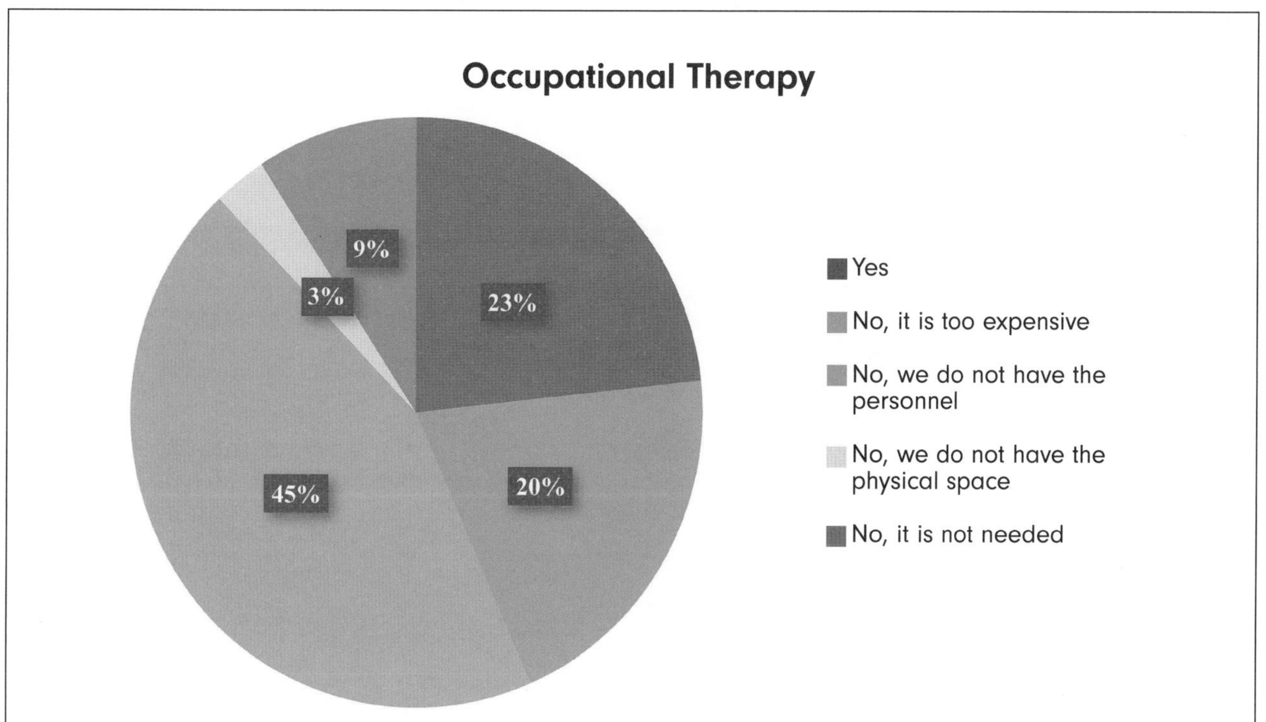

Figure 5.9: Principals Who Report Offering School Psychological Services

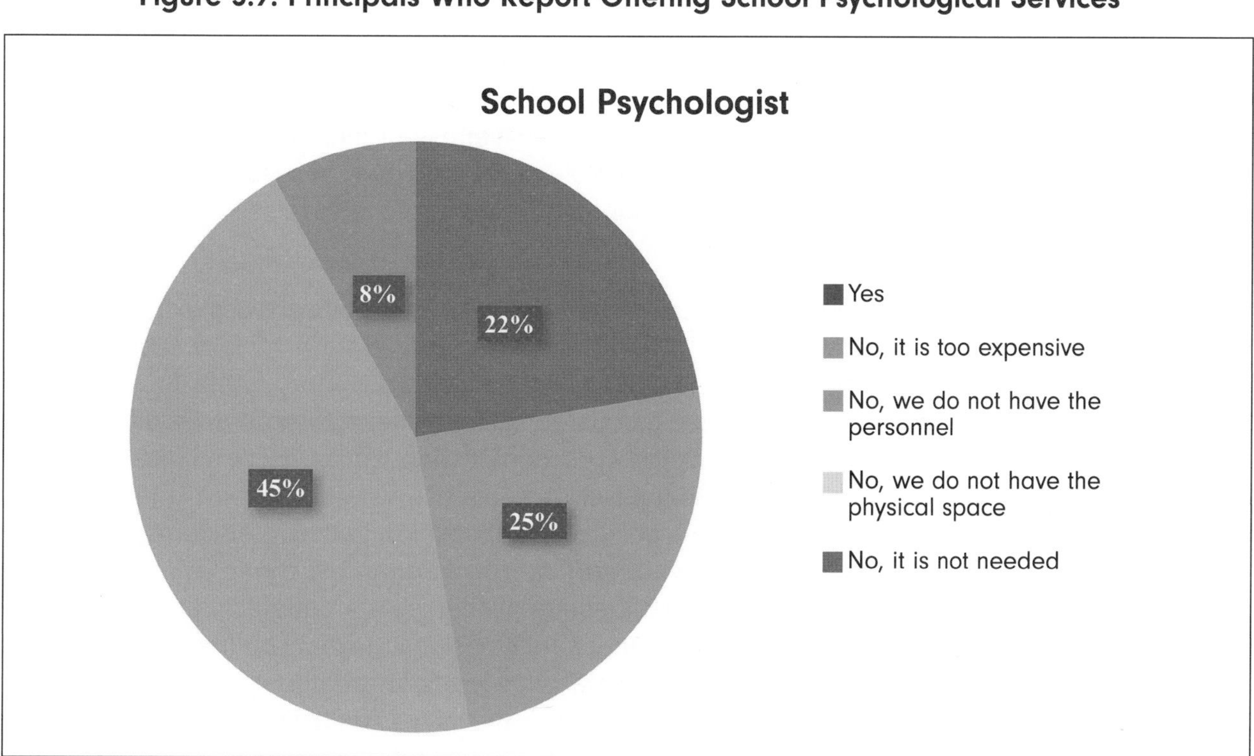

Figure 5.10: Principals Who Report Offering Physical Therapy

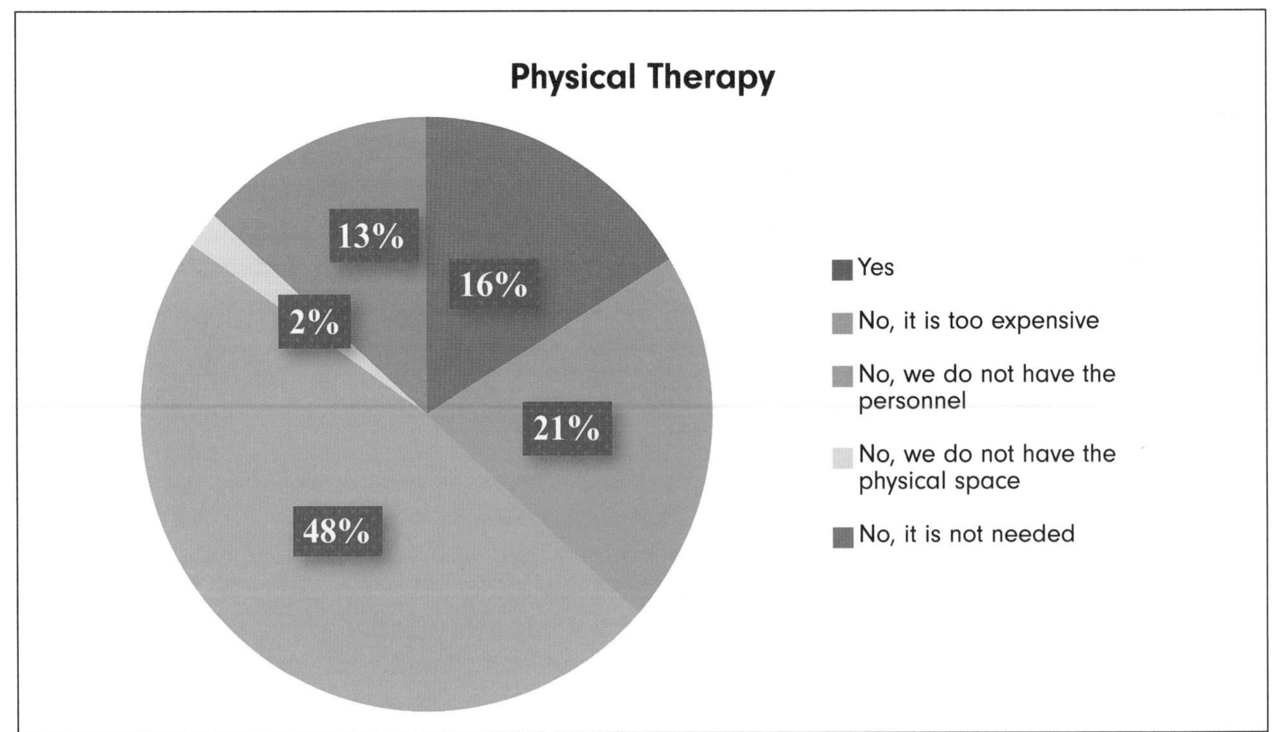

Impact of Supports and Services on Student Outcomes

Understanding the success of interventions and/or services provided for students with disabilities is crucial in evaluating resource management, student growth, and areas of need. Overall, 82 percent of responding principals reported that their schools track the effectiveness of interventions used with their students with disabilities. There were no significant differences by school demographics for responding that there was some way to track the effectiveness of their interventions. Principals reported that teachers were among their most valuable resource when assessing the progress of students with disabilities. In addition to teacher feedback, standardized tests, classroom performance and progress reports also were relied upon heavily.

Principals also were asked to evaluate specifically how the reading and math abilities of their students with disabilities compared to the start of the 2016-17 academic year. Below is information by grade groupings: K-3, 4-8 and high school. Tables 5.1, 5.3, and 5.5 provide a summary of results. Responses to changes in reading and math ability also were compared against other survey data, including school demographics, special education services offered by school, school accessibility by disability type, and professional development opportunities made available to teachers and administrators. This was done in an effort to determine if there were significant relationships between student growth and these school characteristics. ***Where there were significant relationships, those will be reported in tables 5.2 and 5.4.*** It is important to note that these relationships are correlational in nature and that causation was not able to be established for these relationships. It would be inaccurate to state that offering these services or having certain characteristics leads to greater student improvement. These results are simply testing for significant correlations. It also is possible that the characteristics asked about on the survey could be related to other things the school is doing that were not captured in the data. This information is meant to offer opportunities for discussion and further examination.

Grades K-3. Changes in reading ability were assessed for grades K-3. The majority report that reading ability strengthened since the last academic year, with students with autism showing slightly less change than the other students (see Table 5.1).

Table 5.1: Changes in Reading Ability in K-3 by Disability Type (Principal Data)

	Number Responding	Much Stronger	Stronger	No Change	Weaker	Much Weaker
Reading ability for students with an **intellectual/ cognitive disability**	49	14%	71%	10%	4%	–
Reading ability for students with a **learning disability**	63	22%	64%	8%	6%	–
Reading ability for students with **autism**	41	20%	59%	17%	2%	2%

NOTE: % reporting the following measures were used to assess changes in reading ability in K-3: 100% classroom performance; 99% classroom observations, 84% standardized testing; 83% benchmark assessments, and 48% discipline record.

Table 5.2: School Characteristics Related to Changes in Reading Ability for K-3 (Principal Data)

Reading ability for students with an **intellectual/cognitive disability**	– Greater positive change more likely to be seen in schools that offer resource support. – Greater positive change more likely to be seen in schools that offer positive behavior management strategies professional development. – Greater positive change more likely to be seen in schools that offer professional development on the connection between Catholic social teaching and serving students with disabilities.
Reading ability for students with a **learning disability**	– Greater positive change more likely to be seen in schools that offer professional development in understanding special education law.
Reading ability for students with **autism**	– Greater positive change more likely to be seen in schools that offer professional development in understanding special education law.

Grades 4-8. Changes in reading and math ability were assessed for grades 4-8. The majority report that both reading and math strengthened since the last academic year. Similar to the K-3 students, those with autism showed slightly less change than the other students (see Table 5.3).

Table 5.3: Changes in Reading Ability in 4-8 by Disability Type (Principal Data)

	Number Responding	Much Stronger	Stronger	No Change	Weaker	Much Weaker
Reading ability for students with an **intellectual/ cognitive disability**	52	19%	67%	10%	4%	–
Reading ability for students with a **learning disability**	72	19%	65%	8%	7%	–
Reading ability for students with **autism**	45	20%	60%	16%	4%	–
Math ability for students with an **intellectual/ cognitive disability**	52	17%	65%	14%	4%	–
Math ability for students with a **learning disability**	70	17%	63%	14%	6%	–
Math ability for students with **autism**	44	16%	59%	21%	2%	2%

NOTE: % reporting the following measures were used to assess changes in reading ability in 4-8: 99% classroom performance; 97% classroom observations, 88% standardized testing; 81% benchmark assessments, and 50% discipline record.

Table 5.4: School Characteristics Related to Changes in Reading Ability for 4-8 (Principal Data)

Reading ability for students with an **intellectual/cognitive disability**	– Greater positive change more likely to be seen in schools that offer professional development on developing accommodations and modifications to assist students. – Greater positive change more likely to be seen in schools that offer positive behavior management strategies professional development.
Reading ability for students with a **learning disability**	– Greater positive change more likely to be seen in schools that offer professional development on developing accommodations and modifications to assist students. – Greater positive change more likely to be seen in schools that offer professional development on Response to Intervention/Multi-tiered Systems of Support (RtI/MTSS) framework.
Reading ability for students with **autism**	None
Math ability for students with an **intellectual/cognitive disability**	– Greater positive change more likely to be seen in schools that offer professional development on developing accommodations and modifications to assist students.
Math ability for students with a **learning disability**	– Greater positive change more likely to be seen in schools that offer professional development on developing accommodations and modifications to assist students.
Math ability for students with **autism**	None

Grades 9-12. Changes in reading and math ability were assessed for grades 9-12. Compared to the grade school years, there is little perceived change among the high school respondents (see Table 5.5). Due to the low number of respondents and the percent indicating "no change," it was not feasible to analyze any relationships between academic growth and institutional policies and procedures.

Table 5.5: Changes in Reading Ability in 9-12 by Disability Type (Principal Data)

	Number Responding	Much Stronger	Stronger	No Change	Weaker	Much Weaker
Reading ability for students with an **intellectual/ cognitive disability**	9	11%	33%	66%	–	–
Reading ability for students with a **learning disability**	12	8%	50%	42%	–	–
Reading ability for students with **autism**	8	--	63%	38%	–	–
Math ability for students with an **intellectual/ cognitive disability**	9	11%	44%	44%	–	–
Math ability for students with a **learning disability**	12	8%	53%	33%	–	–
Math ability for students with **autism**	8	--	63%	38%	–	–

NOTE: % reporting the following measures were used to assess changes in reading ability in 9-12: 92% classroom performance; 83% classroom observations, 75% standardized testing; 55% discipline record, and 42% benchmark assessments.

Funding

Funding for the needed services comes from a variety of sources. Just over 40 percent of superintendents reported that their diocese helps parish schools find funding through grants and foundations, and 45 percent reported that they seek formalized partnerships with local colleges and universities to help support diocesan schools in serving students with disabilities.

Principals were asked what percent of funding for services comes from a) schools; b) parents or parents' insurance; c) LEA/proportionate plan; or d) other. The majority of funding for services is provided by the schools, with the exception of speech and language services and occupational therapy, which are primarily funded by the LEA/proportionate plan. On average, for example, 59 percent of the funding for resource support is provided by the schools while, on average, 71 percent of the funding for speech and language services is provided by the LEA/proportionate plan. It is important to note that the number of responding principals varies considerably by service type. Therefore, interpretation of these results must be done with caution.

Figure 5.11: Reported Funding sources: Resource Program

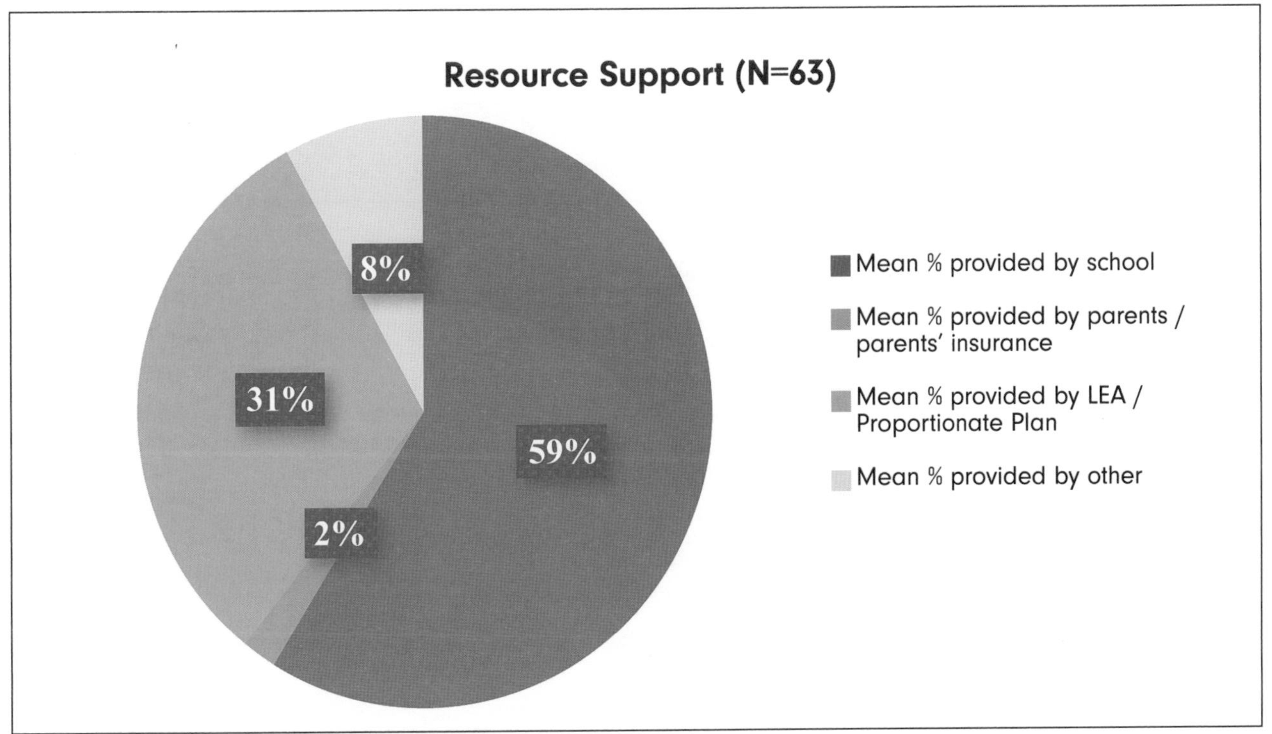

Of the 63 principals reporting this level of programming, 59 percent of the funding was provided by the school while 31 percent of the funding was provided by the local educational agency and 10 percent of the programming came from other sources (see Figure 5.11).

Figure 5.12: Reported Funding Sources: Co-teaching Program

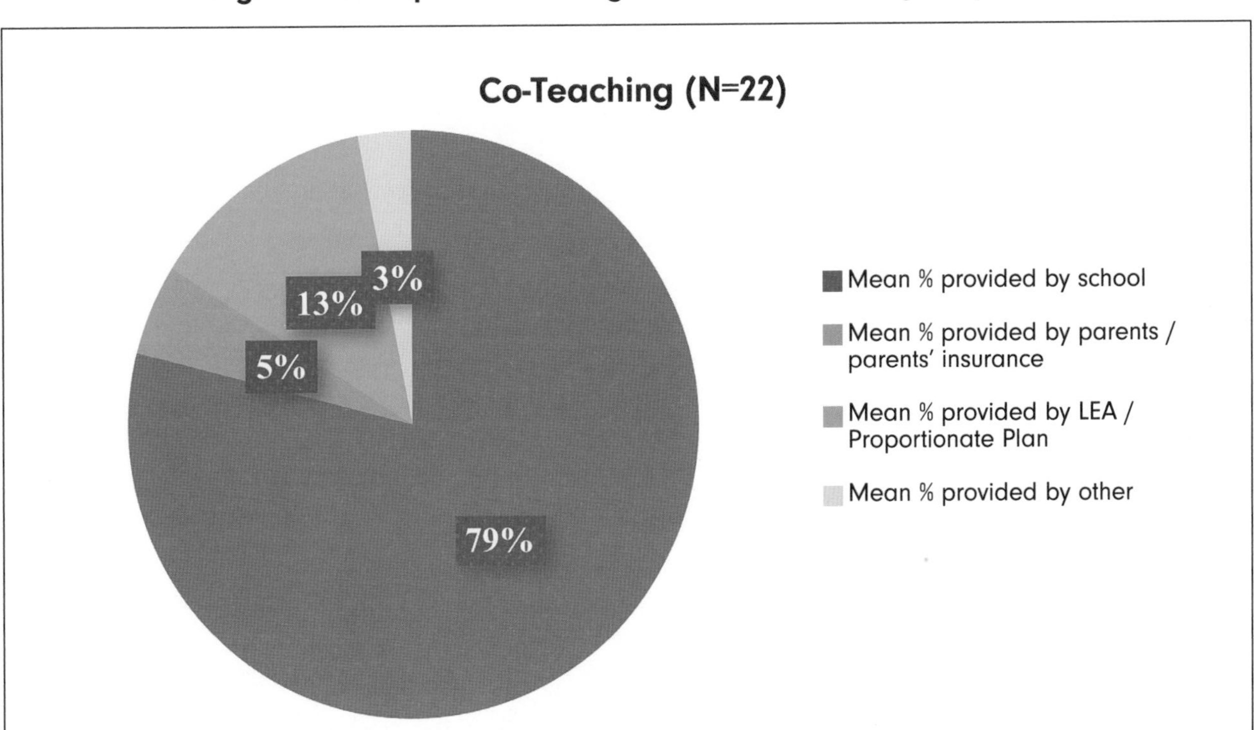

Of the 22 principals with this level of service, 79 percent of the funding was provided by the school while only 21 percent of the funding came from other sources (see Figure 5.12).

Figure 5.13: Reported Funding Sources: Inclusion

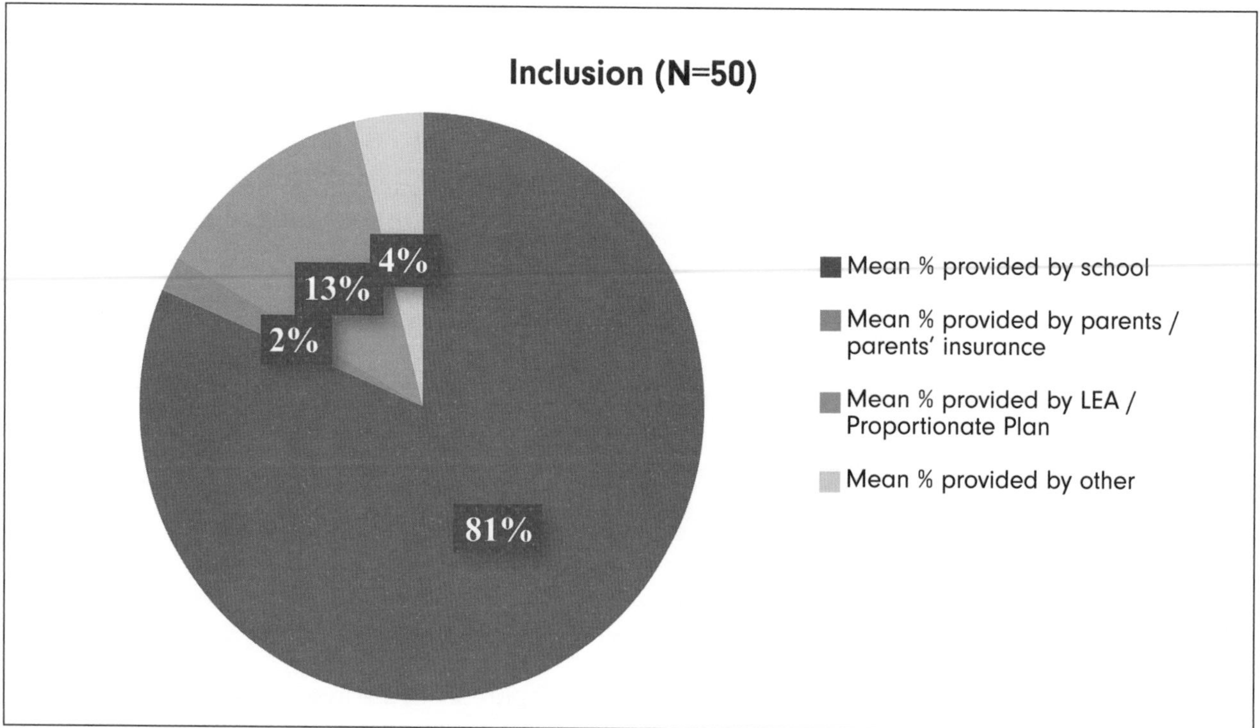

Of the 50 principals in this sample who reported the presence of inclusion programs, 81 percent of the funding was provided by the schools (see Figure 5.13). Principals with this service reported that 13 percent of the funding sources were provided by the local education agency and six percent came from other sources.

Figure 5.14: Reported Funding Source: Special Education Classrooms

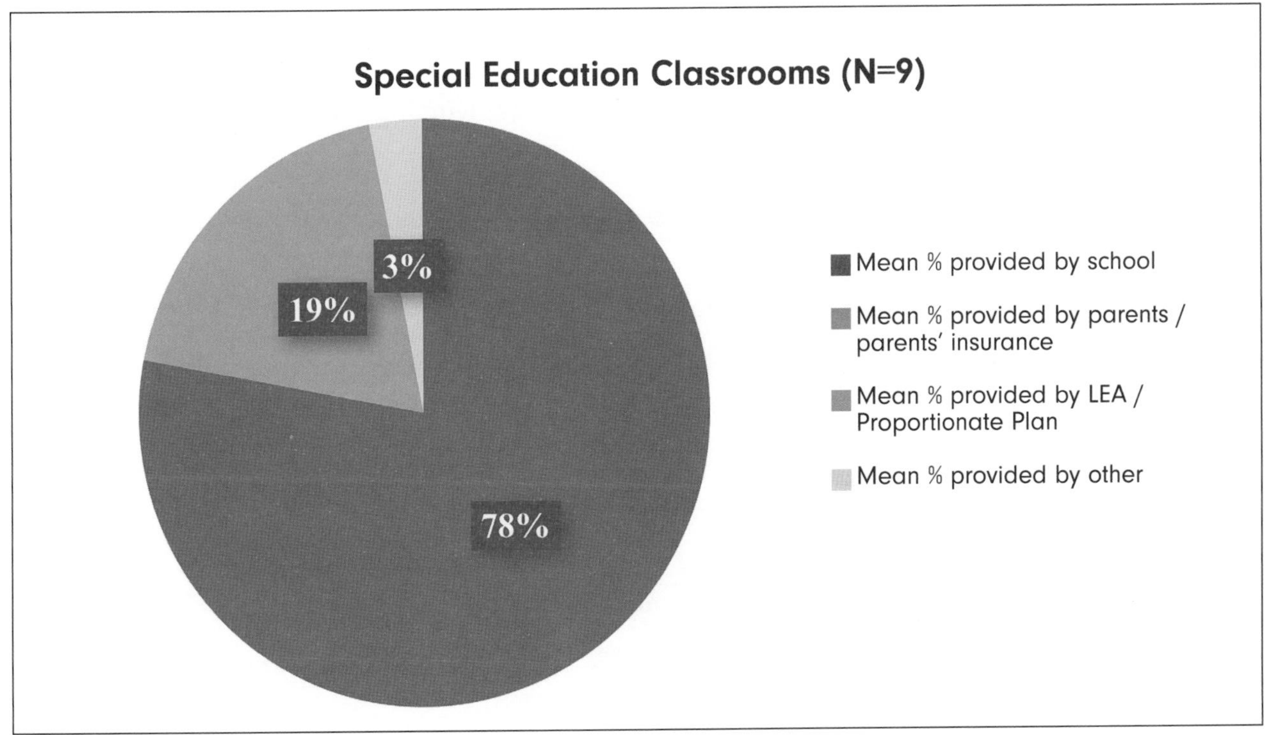

Of the nine principals who reported that they had special classrooms in their schools, 78% of the funding was provided by the school (see Figure 5.14). These principals reported that 19% of the funding was provided by the local educational agency.

Figure 5.15: Reported Funding Sources: Counseling Support

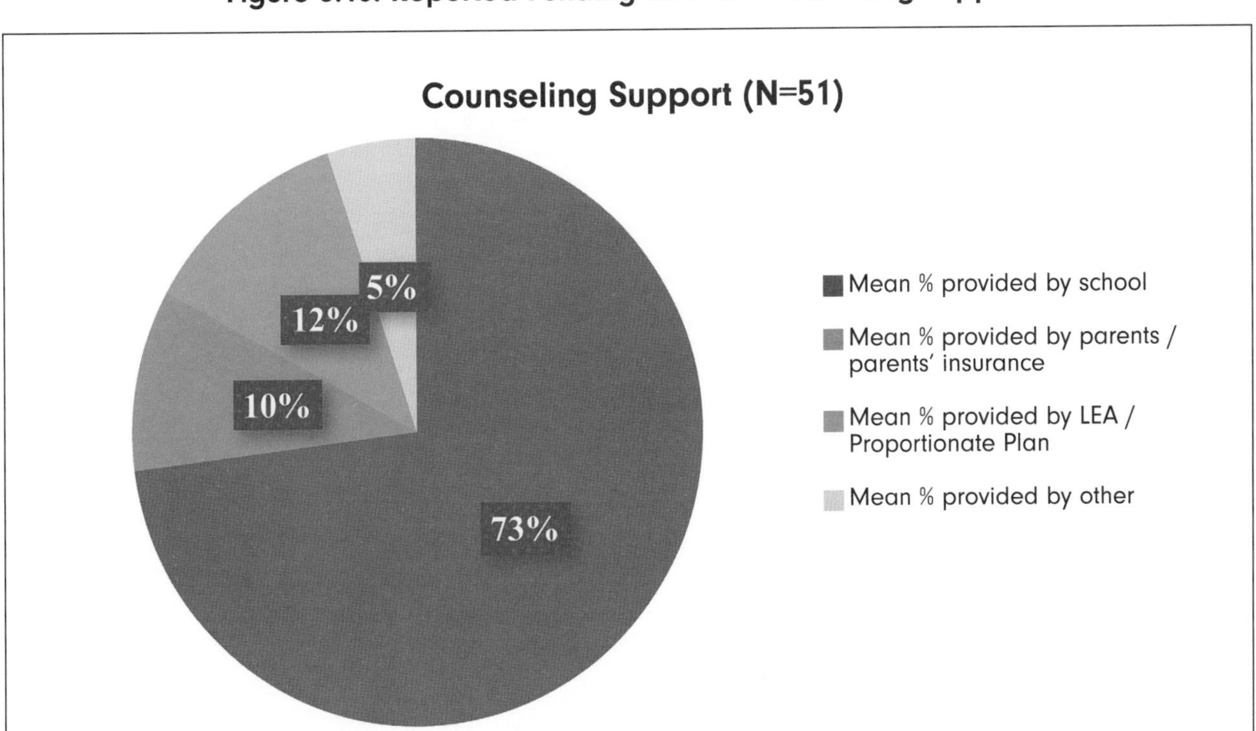

Of the 51 principals who reported this level of programming, 73 percent of the funding was provided by the school, 12 percent was provided by the local agency, and 10 percent was provided by parents (or through their insurance), (see Figure 5.15).

Figure 5.16: Reported Funding Sources: Nursing Support

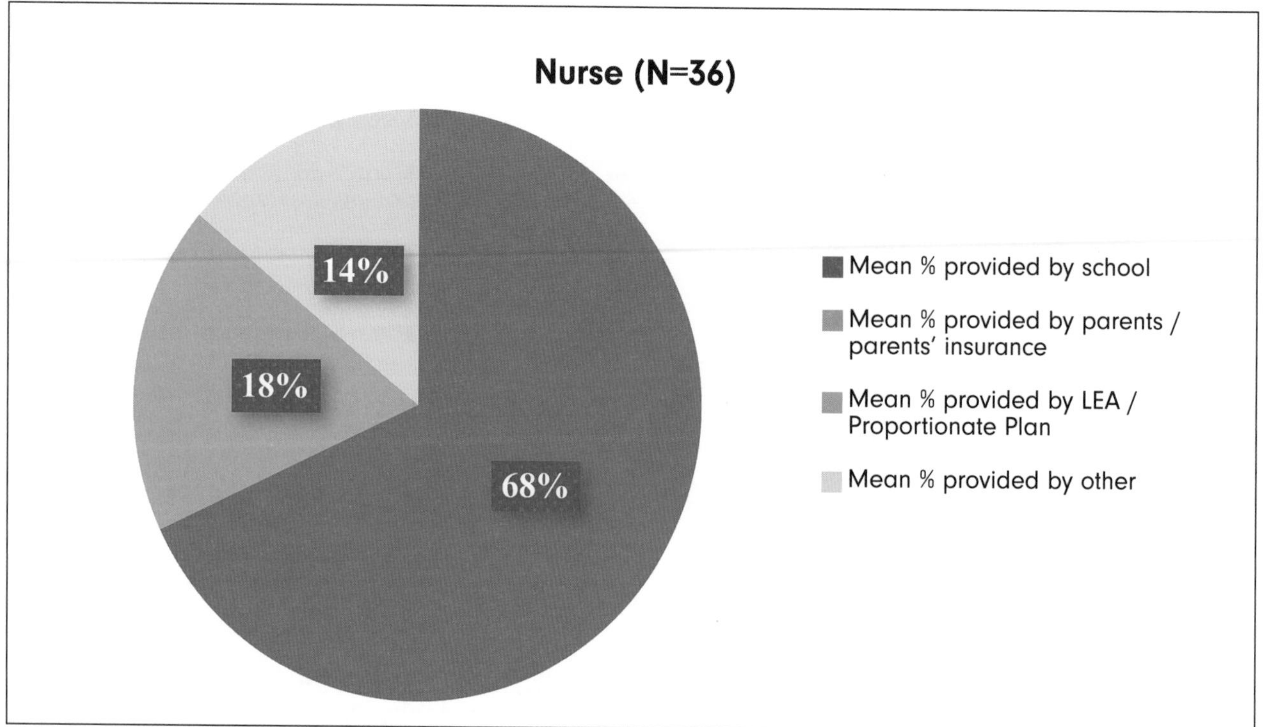

Of the 36 principals who reported this level of service, 68 percent of the funding was through the schools, 18 percent was provided through the local educational agency and 14 percent by other sources (see Figure 5.16).

Figure 5.17: Reported Funding Sources: Paraprofessional

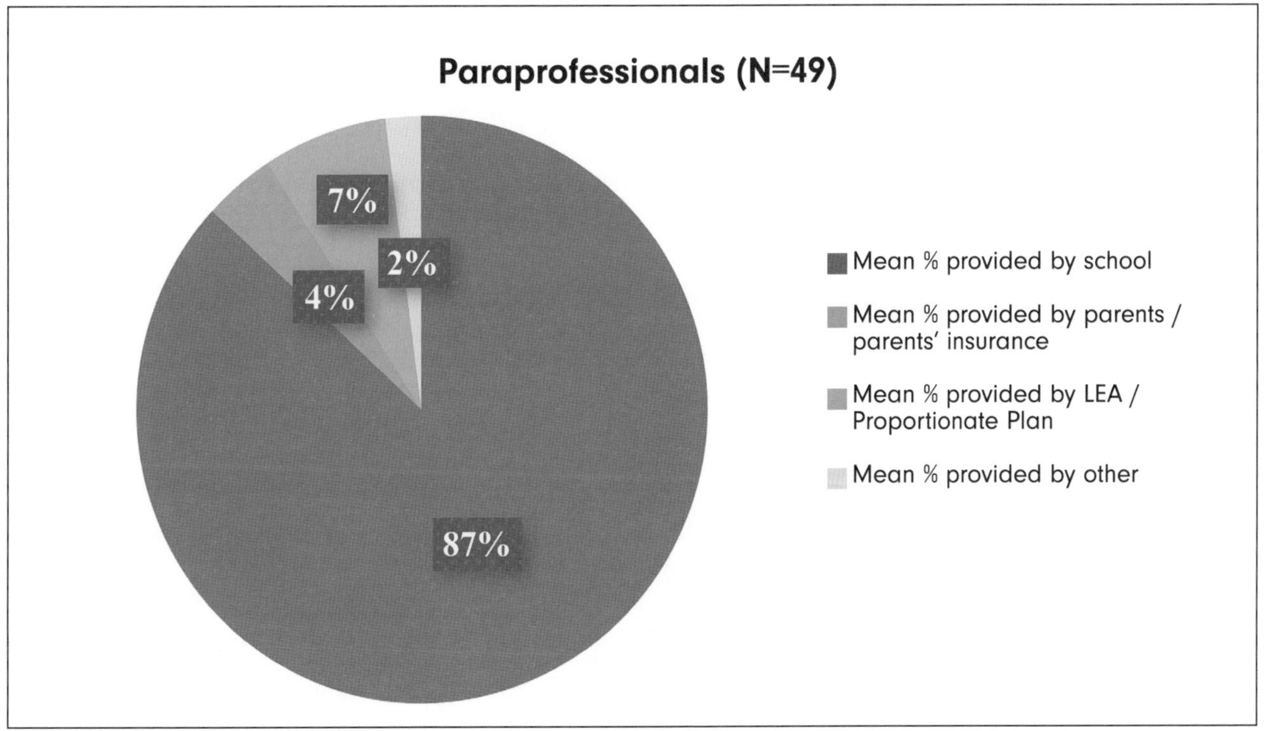

Of the 49 principals reporting this level of service, 87 percent of the funding was provided by the school (see Figure 5.17). It is important to note that schools were overwhelming responsible for this level of funding. Approximately 13 percent of the funding came from other sources.

Figure 5.18: Reports Funding Sources: Speech and Language Services

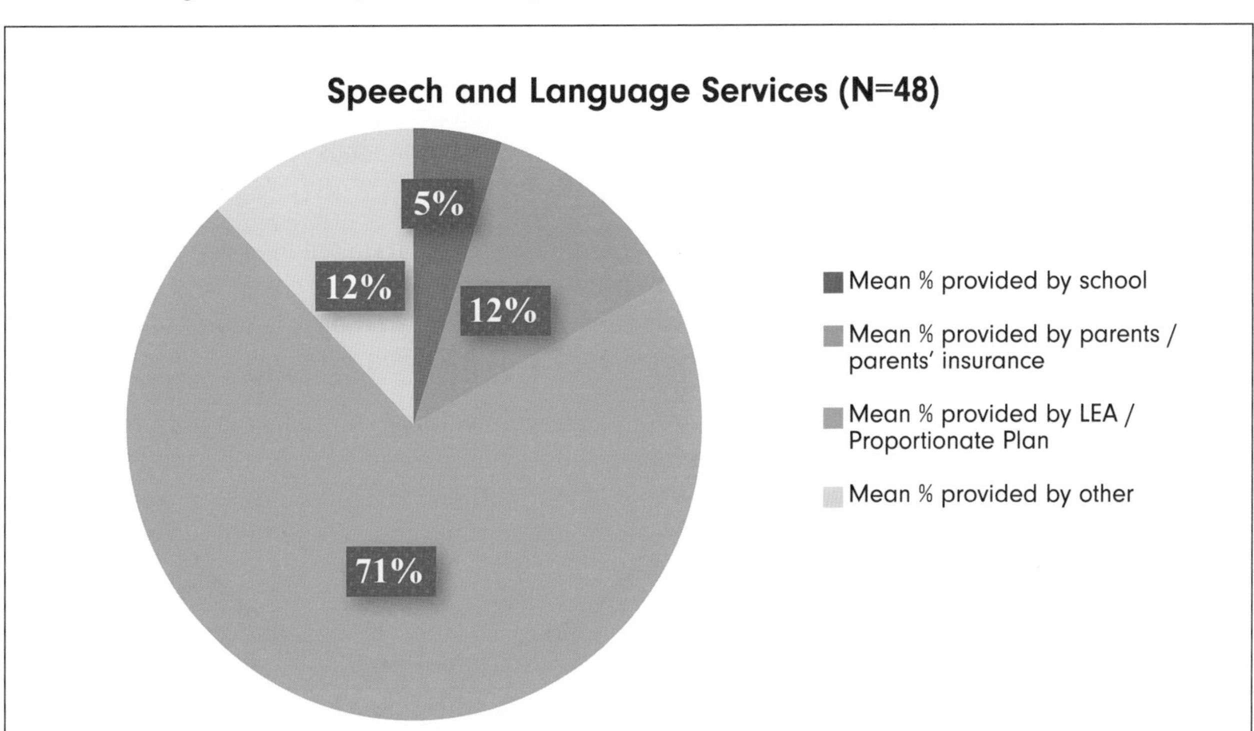

A shift in funding sources was noted in the area of speech and language services. Of the 48 principals who reported this level of services, 71 percent of services were funded by the local educational agency through the proportionate share plan (see Figure 5.18). 12 percent of services were funded by parents (or their insurance) and 12 percent by other sources. Only five percent of services were funded by the school.

Figure 5.19: Reported Funding Sources: Occupational Therapy

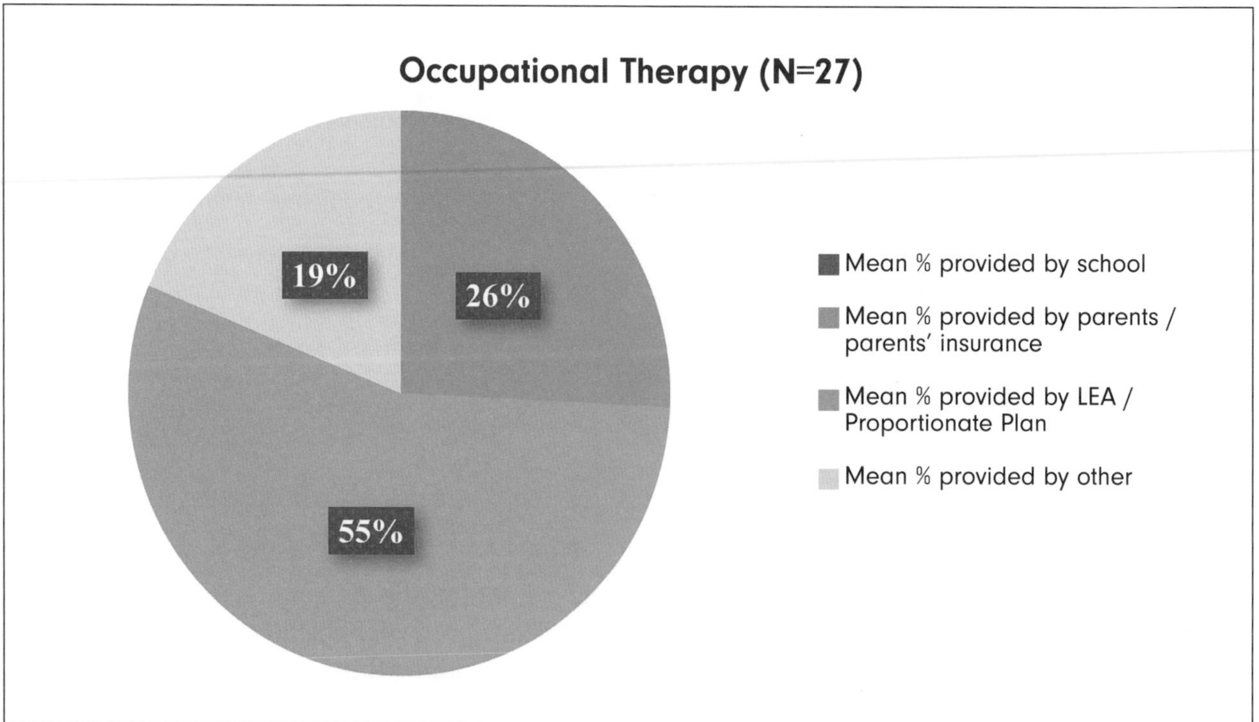

Of the 27 principals reporting this level of service, 55 percent of the funding sources were through the local educational agency through the proportionate share plan (see Figure 5.19). 26 percent of the funding source came from parents (or through the parents' insurance). 19 percent of the funding came through other sources. It should be noted that none of the principals with this level of service reported that the school provided this level of funding.

In regards to other funding sources, 18 percent of the principals reported that their school had sought funding through outside agencies or grant organizations to help cover their costs. And, on average, about six students per school were dually enrolled with the LEA in order to access services. The range, however, extended from 0 students at some schools to 87 at the high end.

Principals also were asked if they or a representative attend the Timely and Meaningful Consultation meetings, where proportionate plans are developed. In total, over three-fourths reported that they or a representative were present. Among those who attended, 50 percent reported being very satisfied or satisfied with the proportionate plans that were developed; another 26 percent were somewhat satisfied, leaving just under one-quarter dissatisfied.

Superintendents also were asked through an open-ended question to describe how the Office of Catholic Schools in their diocese is involved in the development of the proportionate share plans. Responses varied from little involvement and allowing the local schools full autonomy to a detailed collaborative relationship. Many comments mentioned a consultative role for the diocese. One superintendent wrote,

> "As Superintendent of Schools, the "buck stops here." I wrote the Guidance Document that serves as our handbook for students with disabilities. Our office personnel attend workshops, both public and private, that relate to this field, and we share all of that information with our diocesan schools. However, each principal must be the "point guard" for his own building since we lack that personnel role in our office due to staffing and funding restrictions at the diocesan level."

Chapter 6

Challenges and Opportunities

Opportunities for Professional Development: Principals' Survey

With an average of nine percent of a school's population having a disability diagnosis, it is important to understand how the teachers and administrators are being supported and educated to work with this unique population. Principals were asked if their teachers and/or administrators are offered various professional development opportunities.

In terms of understanding disability and its interference with learning (see Figure 6.1), 64 percent of principals noted this was an area that was offered to both administrators and teachers. However, nearly one-third of the respondents noted that this type of professional development was not offered to either administrators or teachers.

Figure 6.1: Principal ratings: Understanding Disabilities and Interference with Learning Results

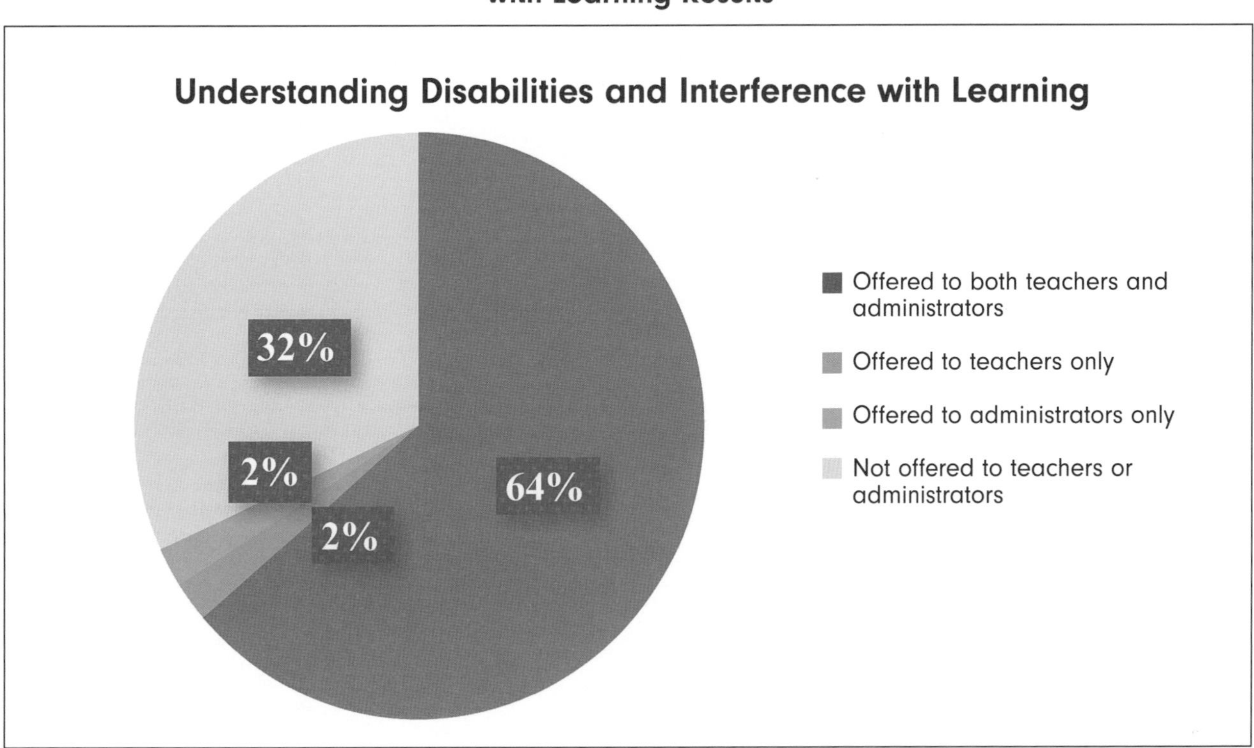

The survey results suggest that much of the professional development provided to teachers and administrators is focused on the practical skills of intervening with students with disabilities. In the area of developing specific skills and strategies (see Figure 6.2) on intervening with students with disabilities, principals reported that this type of training was offered to 3/4 of both teachers and administrators. Additionally, two-thirds of the principal respondents (see Figure 6.3) reported that professional development opportunities regarding developing modifications and accommodations were shared with both teachers and administrators. Finally, two-thirds of principal respondents indicated that professional development opportunities about positive behavioral management strategies (see Figure 6.4) were offered to both teachers and administrators.

Figure 6.2: Principal ratings: Classroom Skills and Strategies

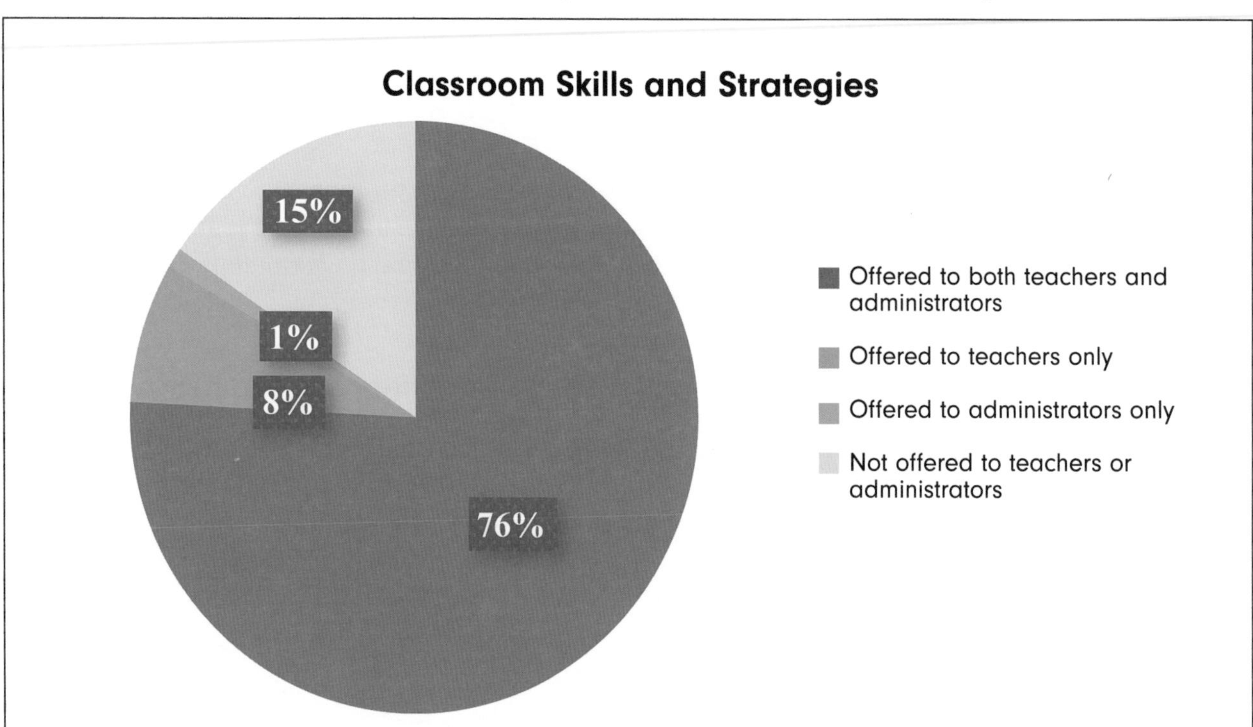

Figure 6.3: Principal Ratings: Developing Modifications and Accommodations

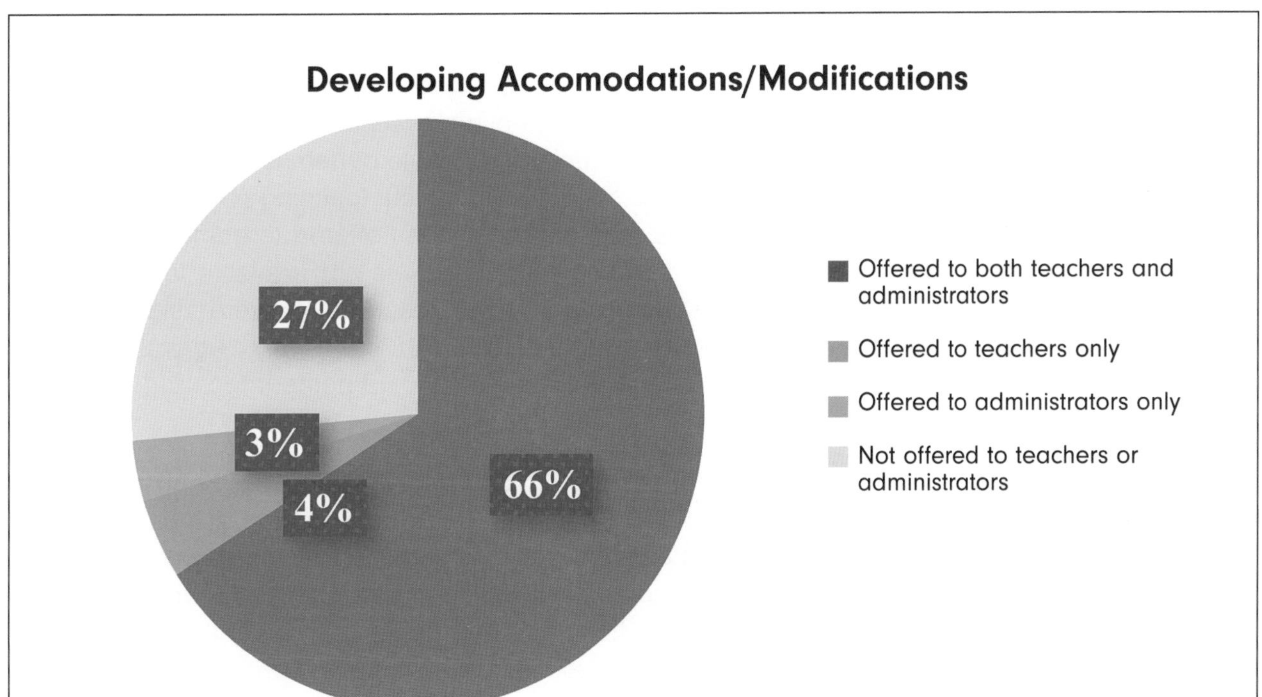

Figure 6.4: Principal Ratings: Positive Behavioral Management Strategies

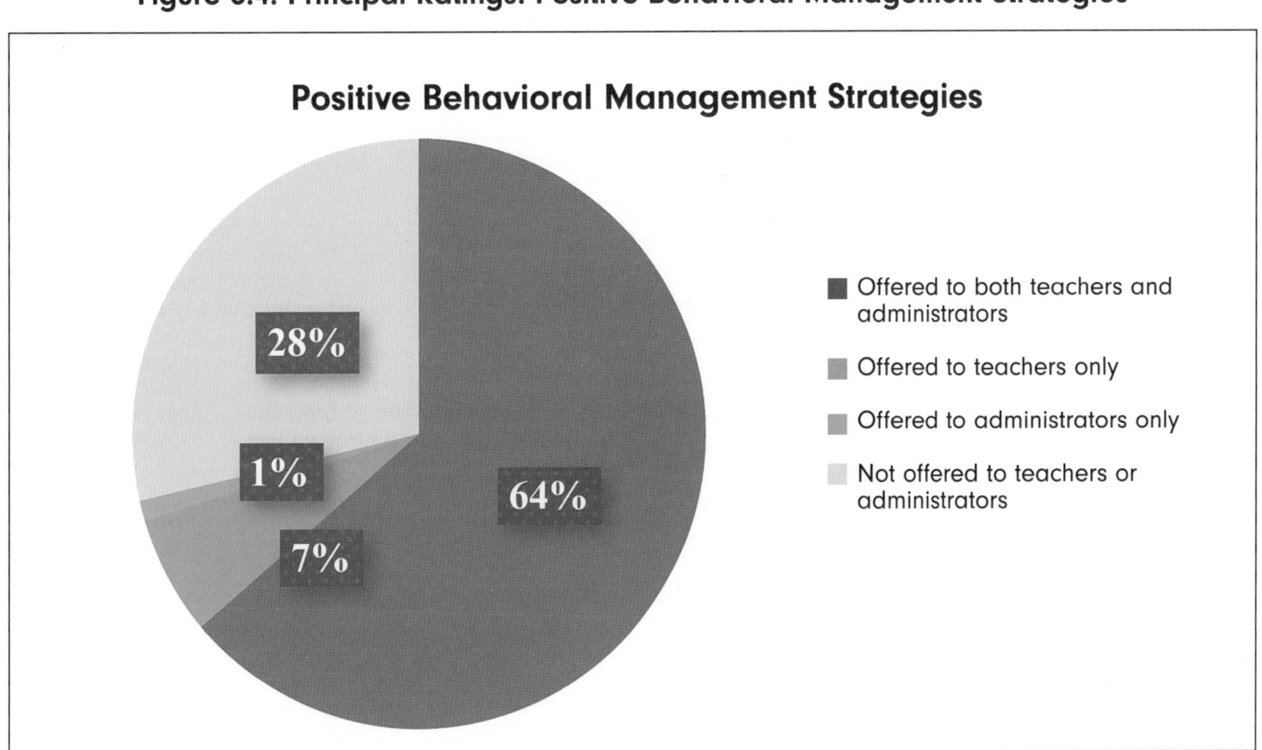

There is a noticeable difference in the reported professional development on topics of special education law (see Figure 6.5) and connection to Catholic Social Teaching (see Figure 6.6) and understanding Response to Intervention/Multi-tiered Systems of Support (RtI/MTSS) (see Figure 6.7). The survey suggests a nearly even split with 42 percent of administrators receiving professional development on special education law, while 35 percent reported that neither teachers nor administrators have received this type of professional development opportunity. This same pattern is found in connecting servicing students with disabilities with the themes of Catholic Social Teaching (CST). Forty-seven (47) percent of respondents suggested that this type of training was offered to administrators only and 47 percent of respondents reported that this type of training was not available to teachers or administrators. This same kind of finding was also evident when respondents were asked to report professional development opportunities related to using the RtI/MTSS framework. Again, 47 percent of principals reported that this was offered to administrators only and 43 percent reported that it was not offered to administrators or teachers.

This suggests an opportunity. These three areas really constitute the "why" of serving students with disabilities in Catholic schools. Understanding the legal framework around special education helps staff learn ways to advocate for their students as well as maximize existing resources for their buildings. The RtI/MTSS framework can help unify existing support structures as well as provide a systematic approach to utilizing evidenced practices that can benefit all students (Boyle, 2010). Finally, specific professional development on the relationship between CST and programming for students with disabilities provides the ultimate rationale for why this should be done. By creating an understanding of why Catholic schools should address the needs of those with disabilities, school staffs are better equipped to address the bishops' call for inclusion (NCCB, 1978).

Figure 6.5: Principal Ratings: Special Education Law

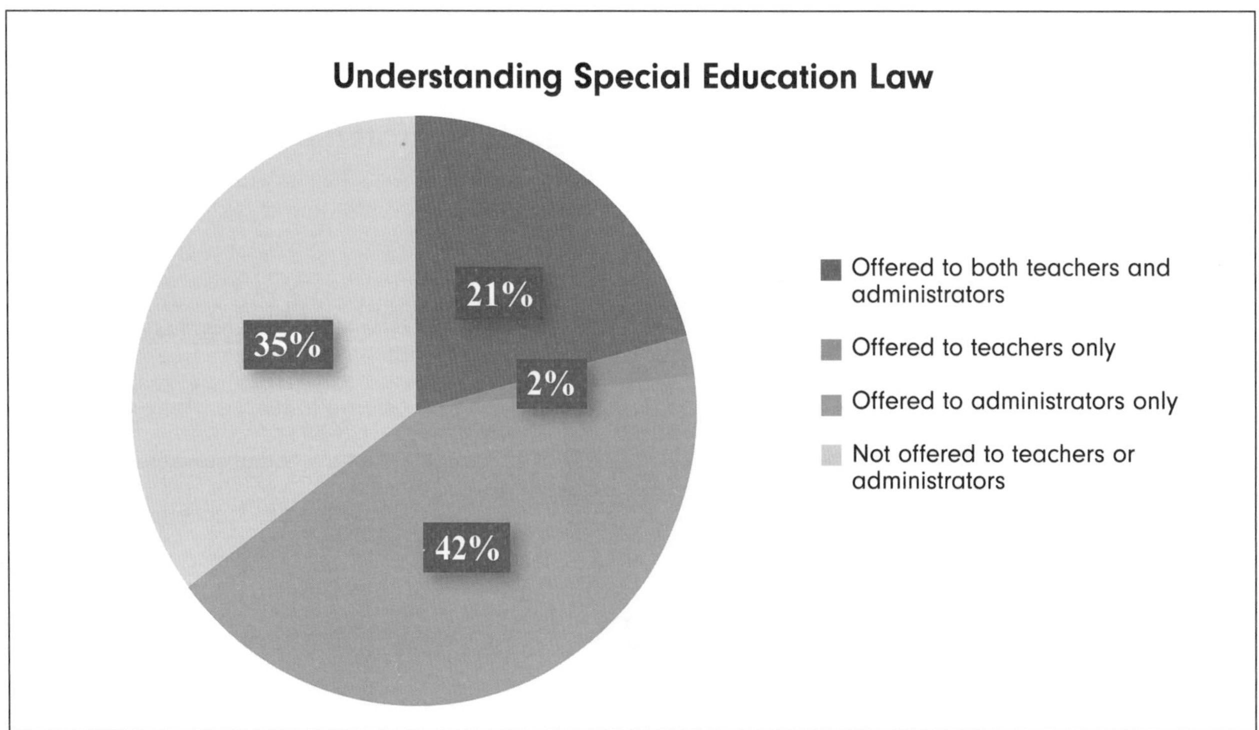

Figure 6.6: Principal Ratings: Connection to Catholic Social Teaching

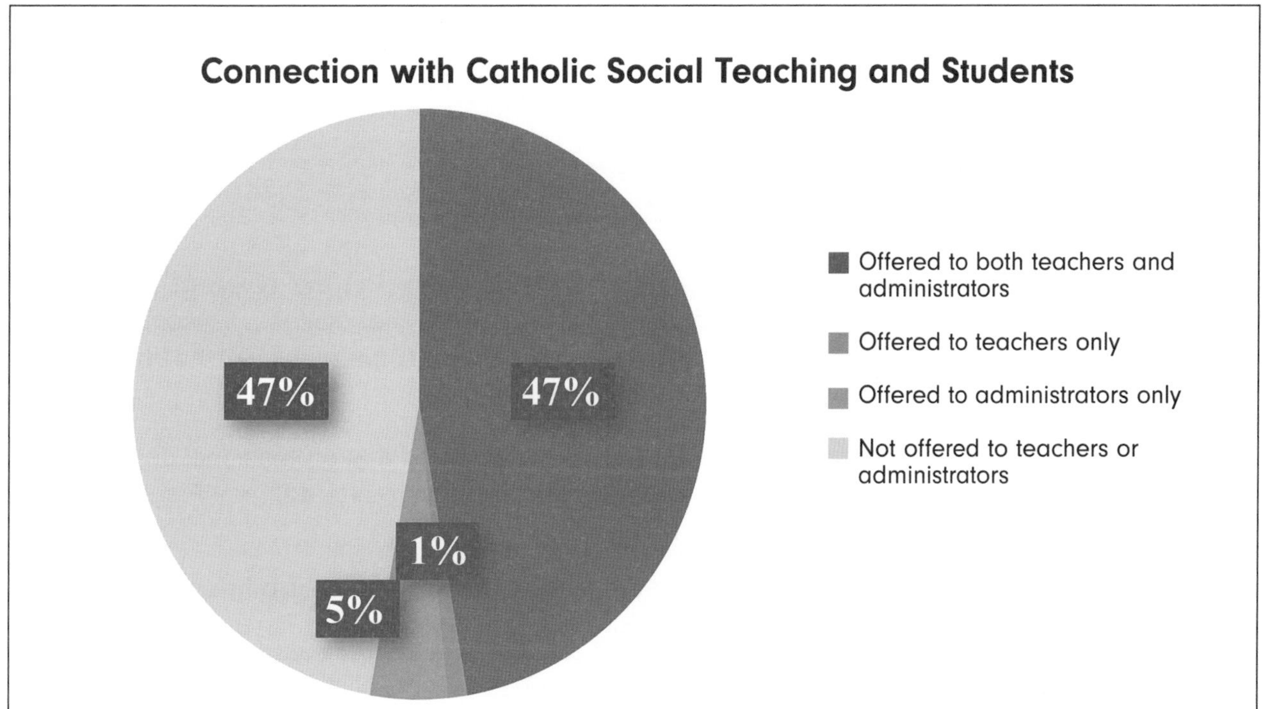

Figure 6.7: Principal ratings: RTI/MTSS Framework

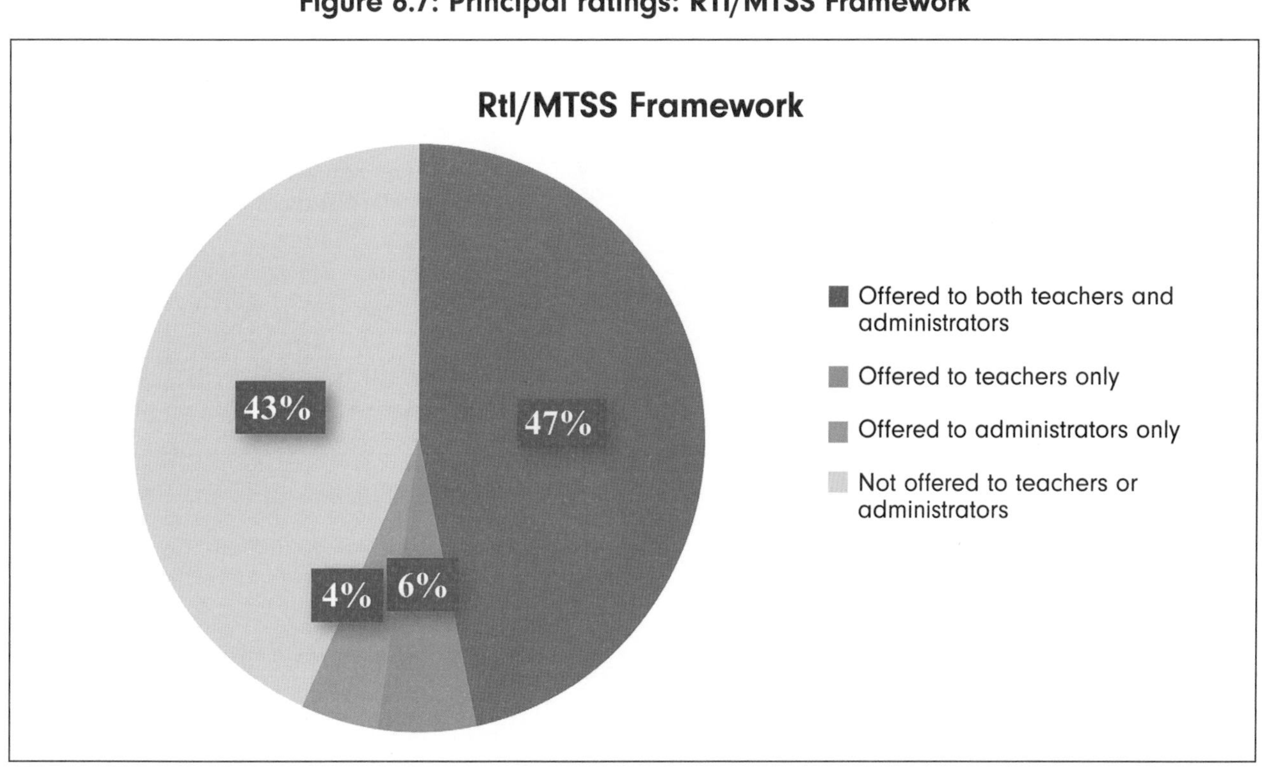

There were few differences when examining professional development opportunities by school demographics. Just two emerged. Schools that service elementary grades as opposed to high schools were more likely to report that teachers and/or administrators were offered professional development in special education law and positive behavioral management strategies.

Opportunities for Professional Development: Superintendents' Survey

On the superintendents' survey, respondents were asked to report on the types of professional development that they offer to teachers and administrators of the diocese. According to the superintendents' survey, at least one-half of the dioceses represented offered each of the opportunities to their teachers and/or administrators (see Figures 6.8-6.14).

Approximately two-thirds of the superintendent respondents reported that professional development, regarding understanding disabilities and their impact on learning, were offered. (see Figure 6.8).

Figure 6.8: Superintendent Responses: Understanding Disabilities and Interference with Learning Results

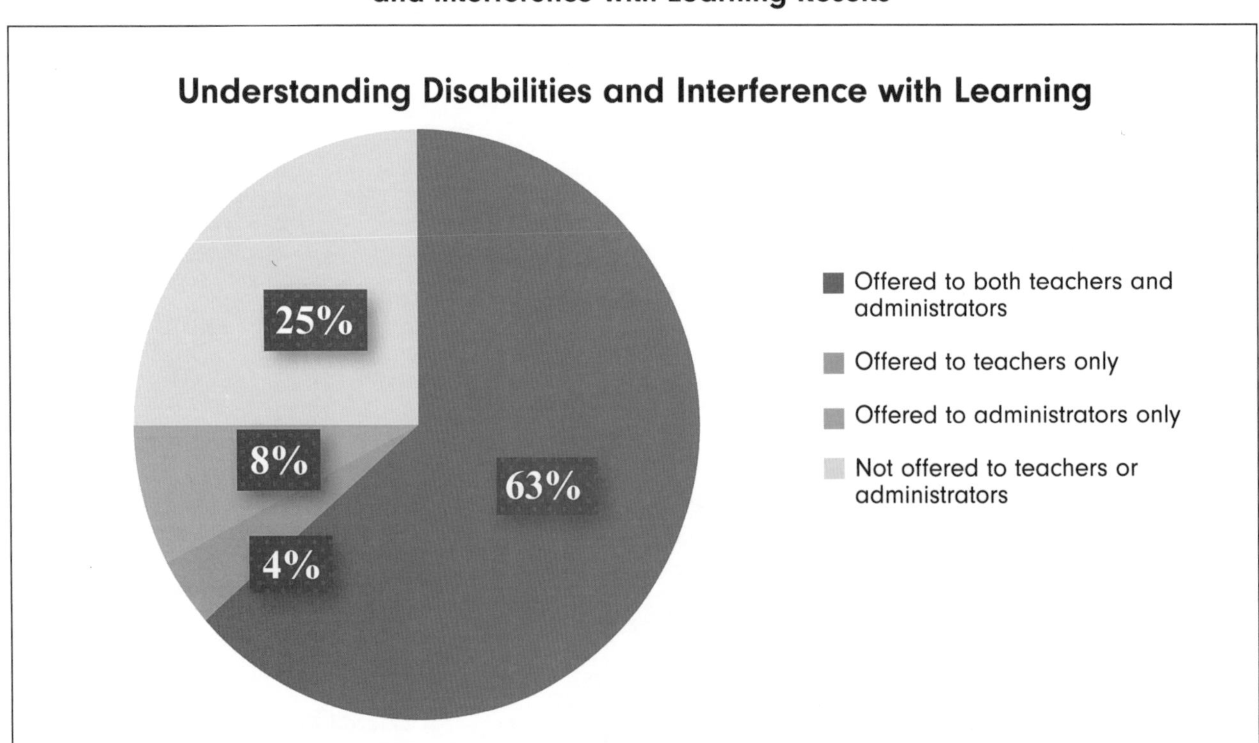

Much like the responses from the principal survey, the superintendents reported that professional development provided to teachers and administrators was focused on the practical skills of intervening with students with disabilities. Eighty-three (83) percent of superintendent respondents noted that professional development was offered to teachers and administrators about classroom skills and strategies for instructing students with disabilities (see Figure 6.9). Sixty-one (61) percent of the superintendent respondents reported that teachers and administrators were offered professional development about developing modifications and accommodations for students with disabilities (see Figure 6.10). Finally, 54 percent of superintendent respondents reported that teachers and administrators were offered professional development related to positive behavioral management strategies (see Figure 6.11).

Figure 6.9: Superintendent Responses: Classroom Skills and Strategies

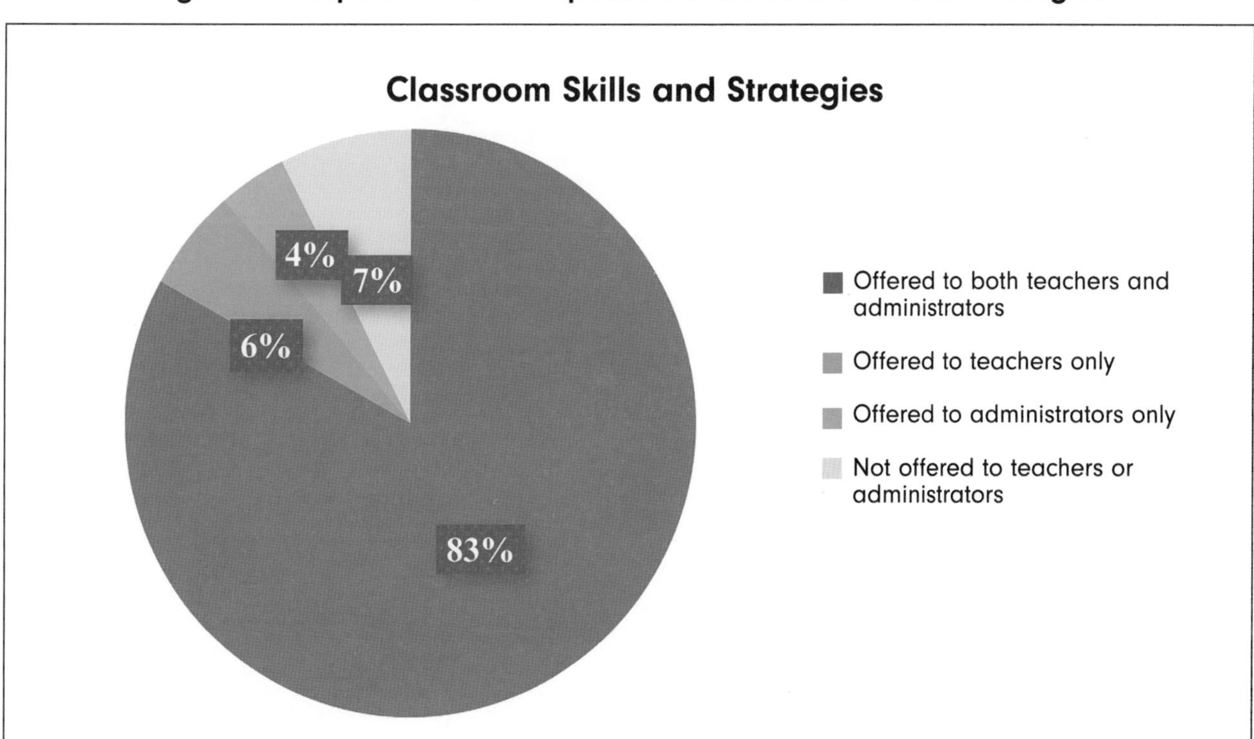

Figure 6.10 Superintendent responses: Developing Modifications and Accommodations

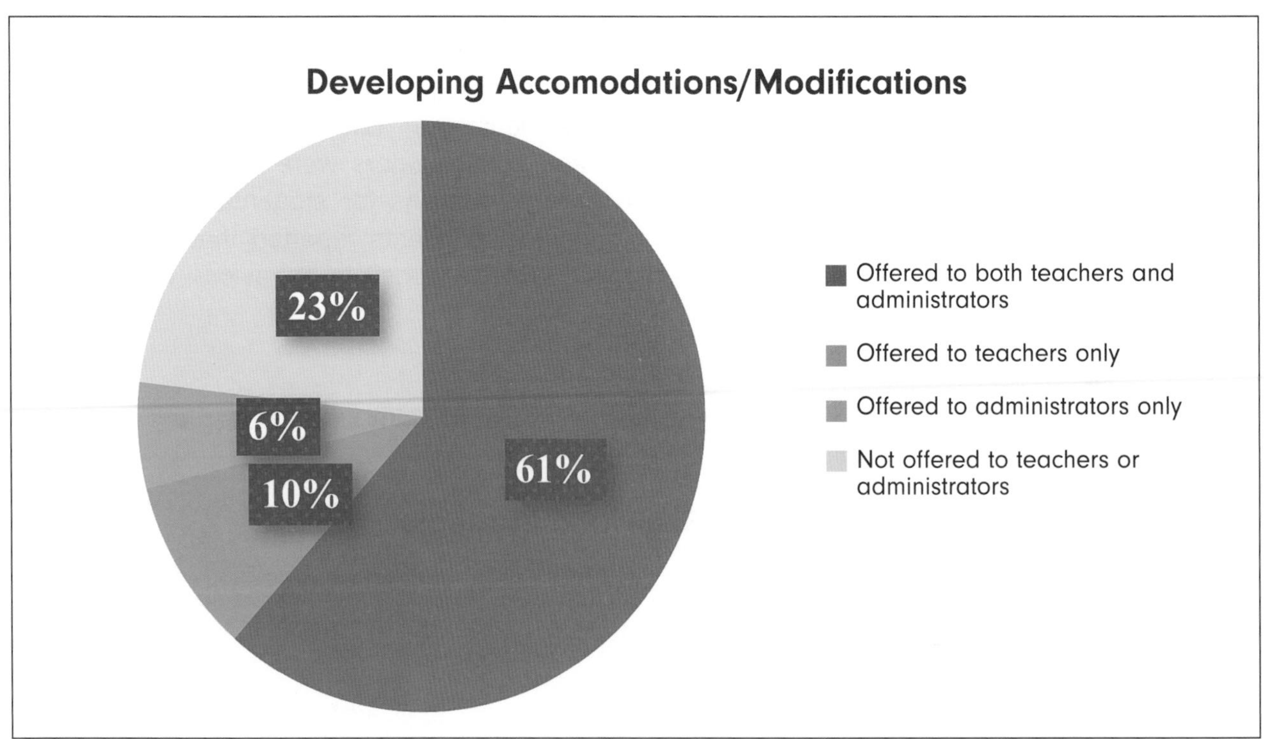

Figure 6.11: Superintendent Responses: Positive Behavioral Management Strategies

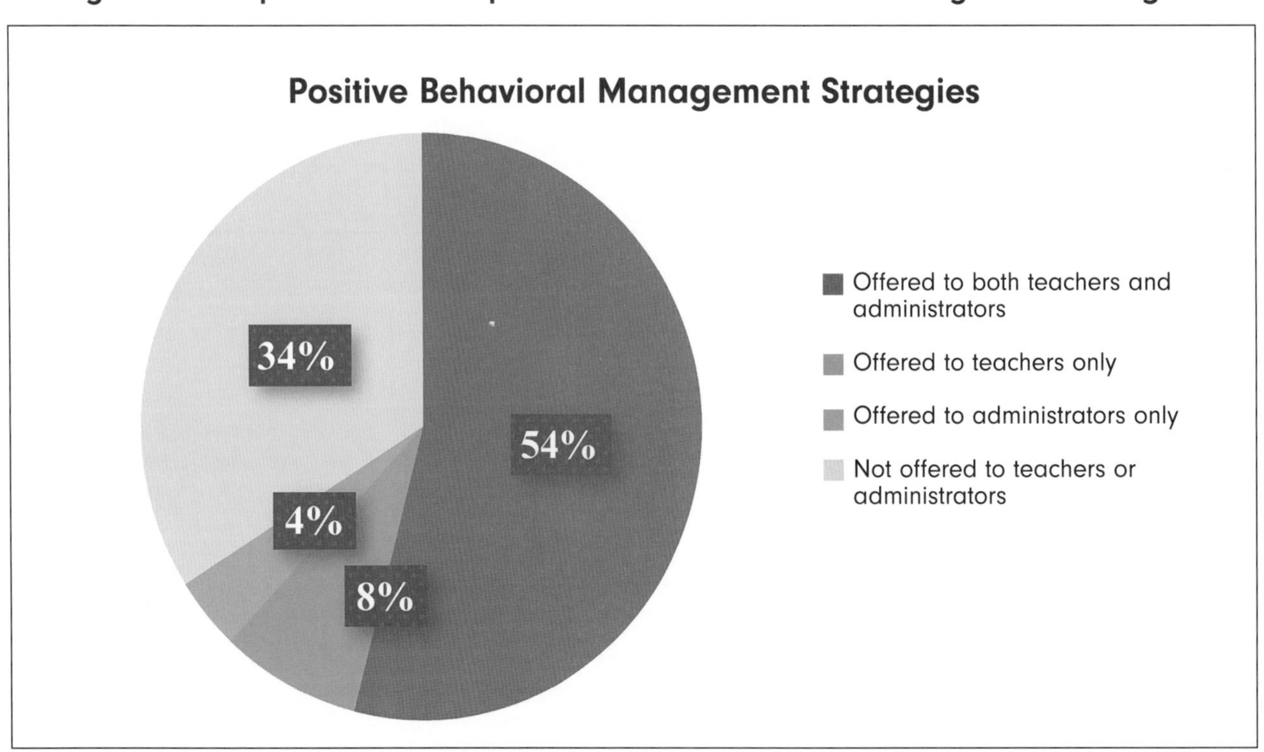

In the area of special education law, roughly one-third of superintendent respondents reported that teachers and administrators were offered professional development related to this area, while one-third reported that administrators received these professional development opportunities (see Figure 6.12). The final third reported that neither teachers nor administrators received this kind of training. This is an area of opportunity to support teachers and school leaders.

Figure 6.12: Superintendent Responses: Special Education Law

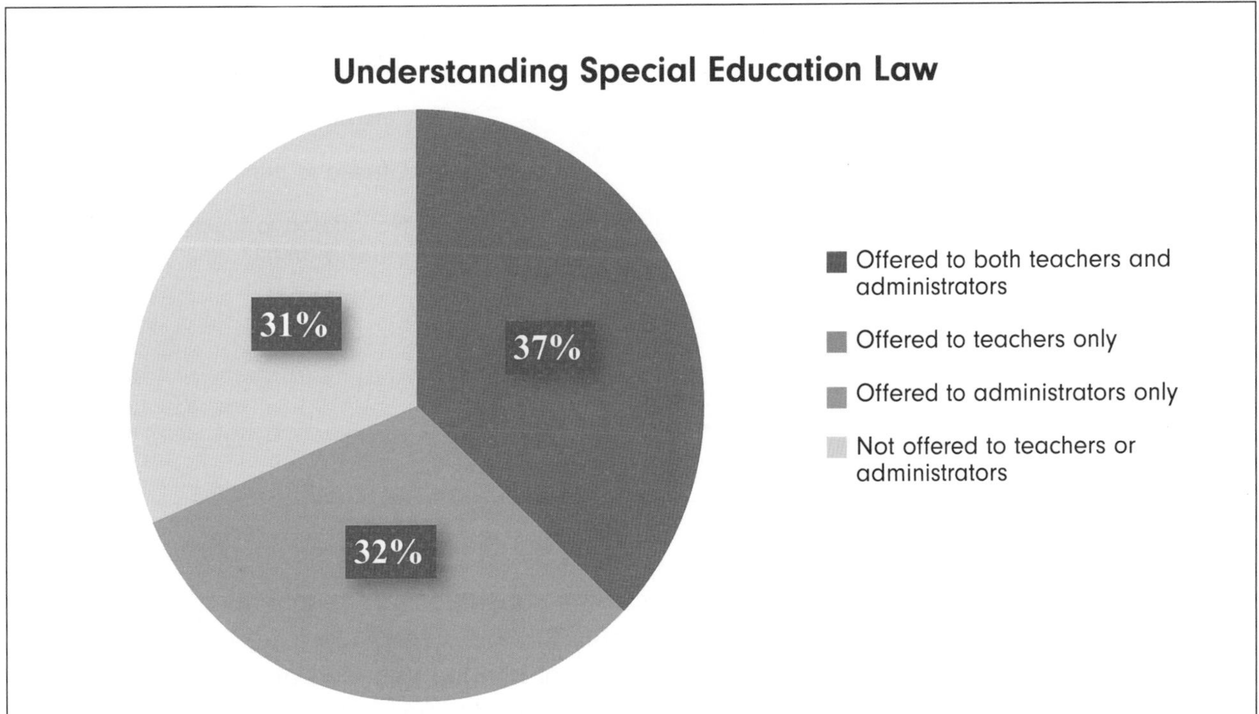

In the area of connecting serving students with disabilities to Catholic Social Teaching, only 39 percent of the superintendents reported offering this kind of professional development to teachers and administrators (see Figure 6.13). It is interesting to note that 45 percent of the superintendent respondents reported that this kind of opportunity was not offered to either teachers or administrators. It appears that this might be a golden opportunity to support teachers and leaders.

Figure 6.13: Superintendent Responses: Connection to Catholic Social Teaching

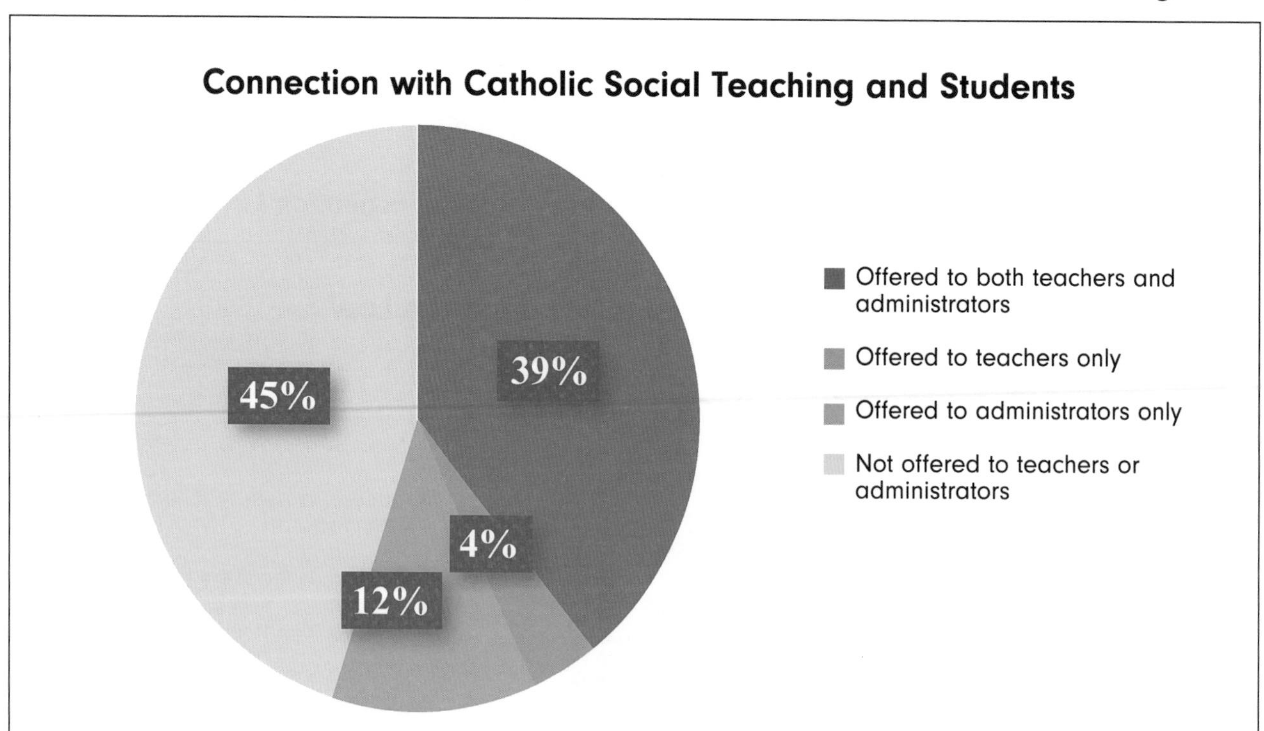

Finally, in the area of RtI/MTSS, only 40 percent of the superintendent respondents noted offering professional development to both teachers and administrators. (see Figure 6.14). Nearly half (44 percent) of the superintendent respondents reported not offering this kind of opportunity to either teachers or administrators. This is another area of opportunity to support teachers and leaders.

Figure 6.14: Superintendent Responses: RTI/MTSS Framework

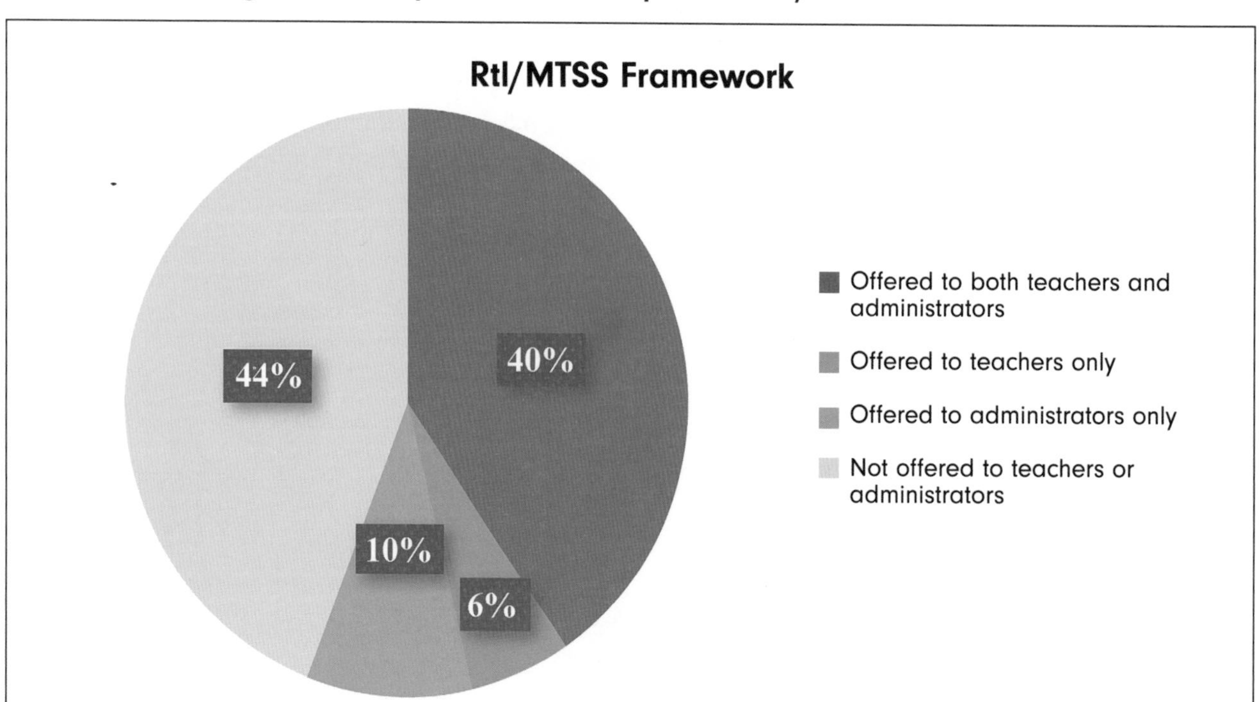

Perceptions of School Staff Strengths and Areas to Grow

Finally, principals were asked to assess their capacity in a variety of areas involving supporting students with disabilities (see Figures 6.15-6.22). Principals generally reported that their teaching staff and administrators were trained and equipped to meet the educational needs of those students with disabilities. There is, however, room for growth in every area discussed, but especially in teachers and administrators understanding root cause analysis and teachers understanding the Response to Intervention/Multi-tiered Systems of Support (RtI/MTSS) framework.

Figure 6.15: Principal Report of Administrators' Understanding of Root Cause Analysis

Our Administrators Have a Firm Understanding of Root Cause Analysis

15%
7%
22%
19%
14%
23%

Strongly Agree
Agree
Somewhat Agree
Somewhat Disagree
Disagree
Strongly Disagree

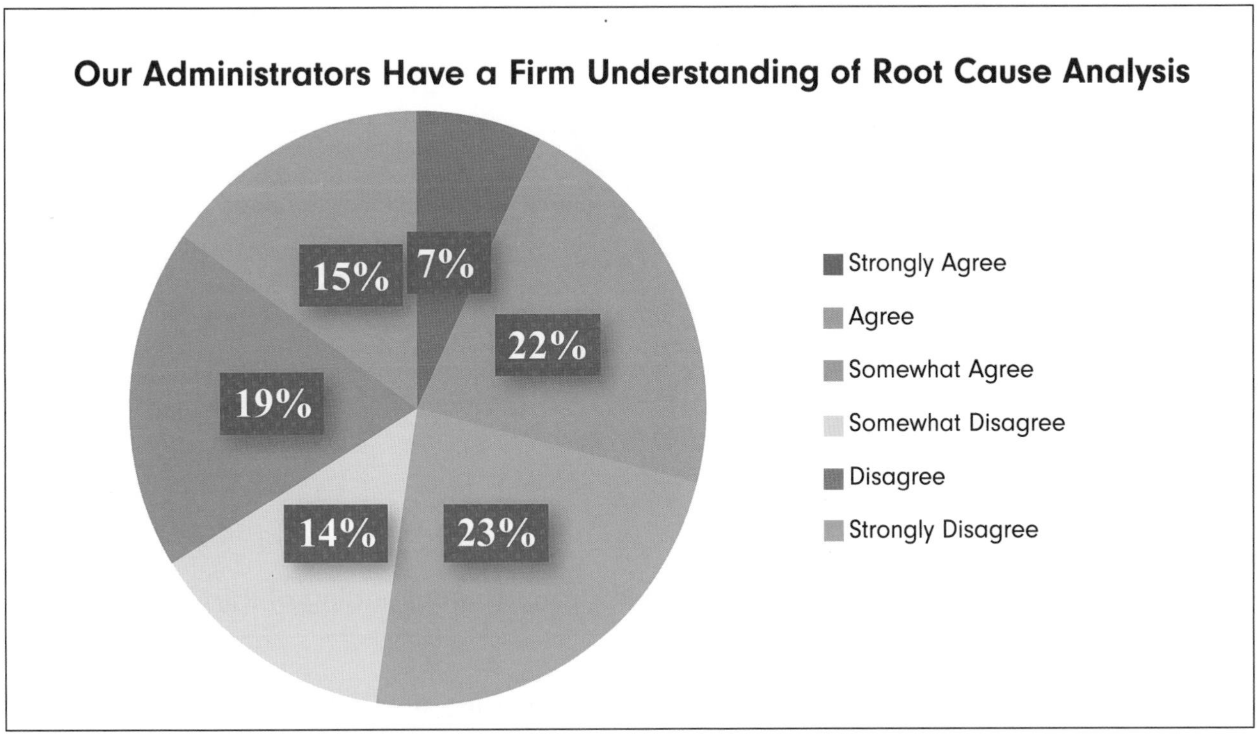

Figure 6.16: Principal Report of Teacher Understanding of Root Cause Analysis

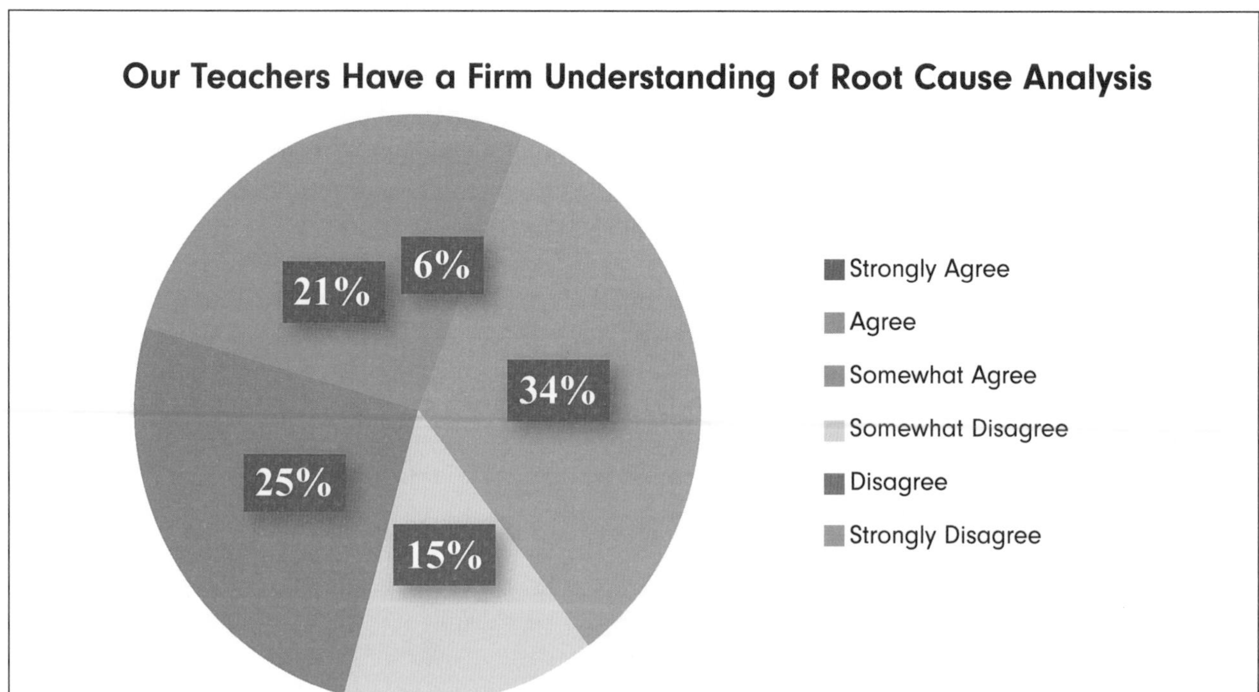

Figure 6.17: Principal Report of Administrator Understanding of RtI/MTSS

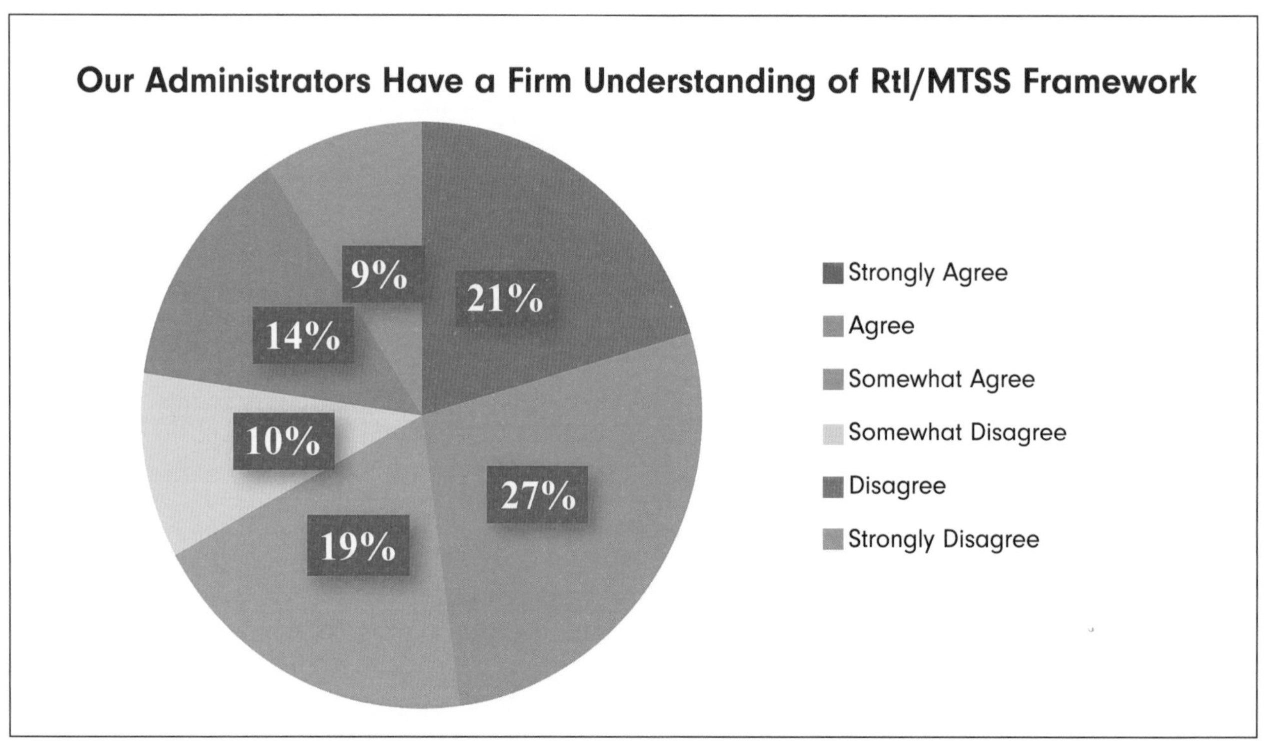

Figure 6.18: Principal Report of Teacher Understanding of RtI/MTSS

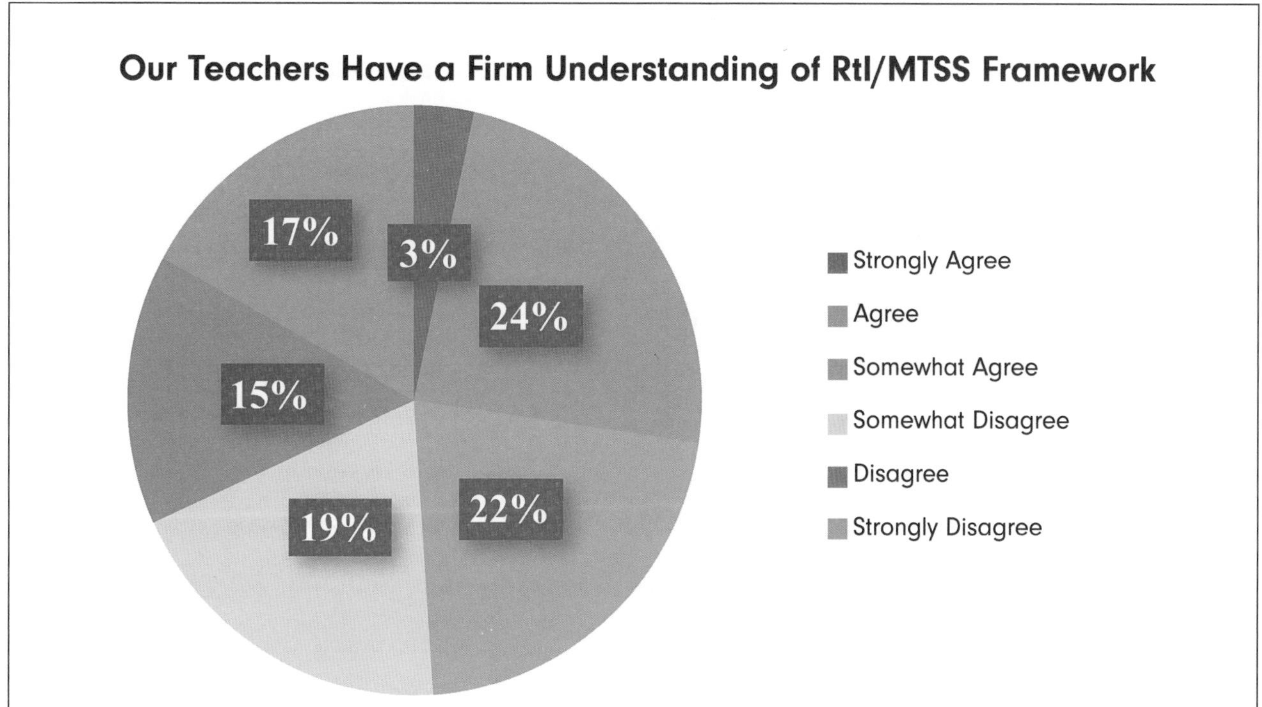

Figure 6.19: Principal Report of Ability to Assess Growth of Students with Disabilities

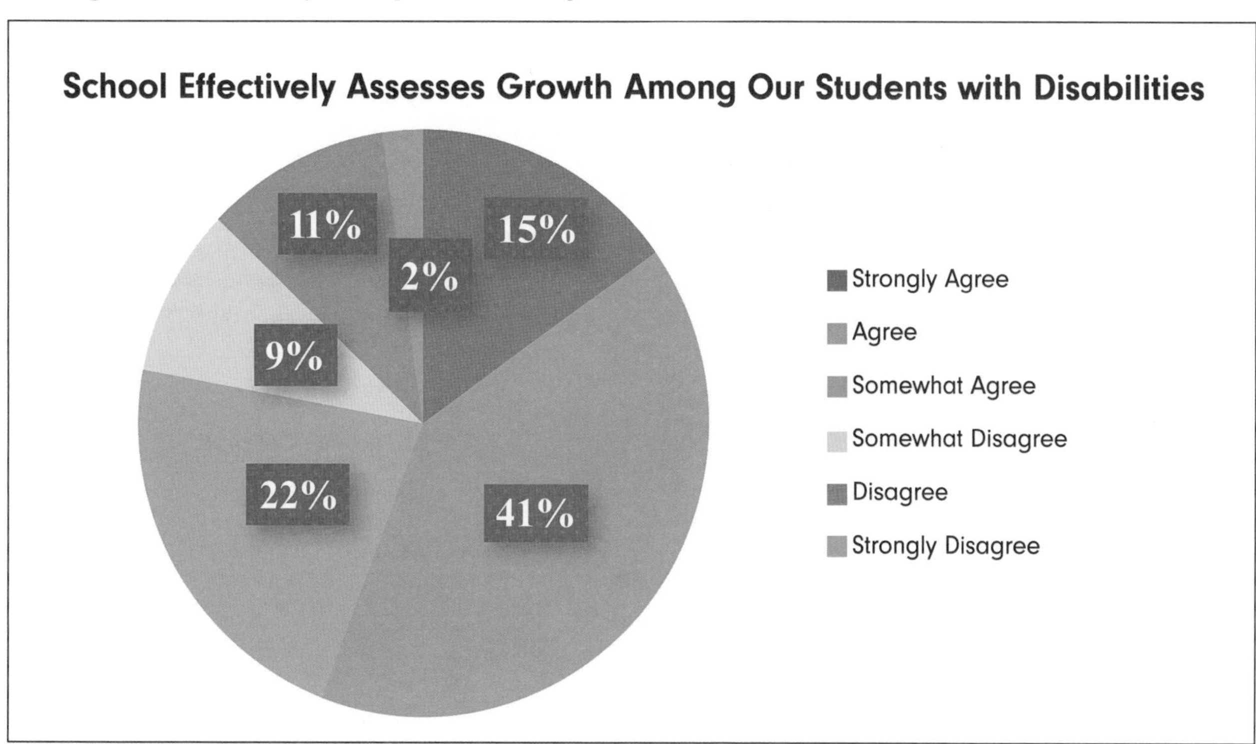

Figure 6.20: Principal Report of Administrator Understanding of Special Education Law

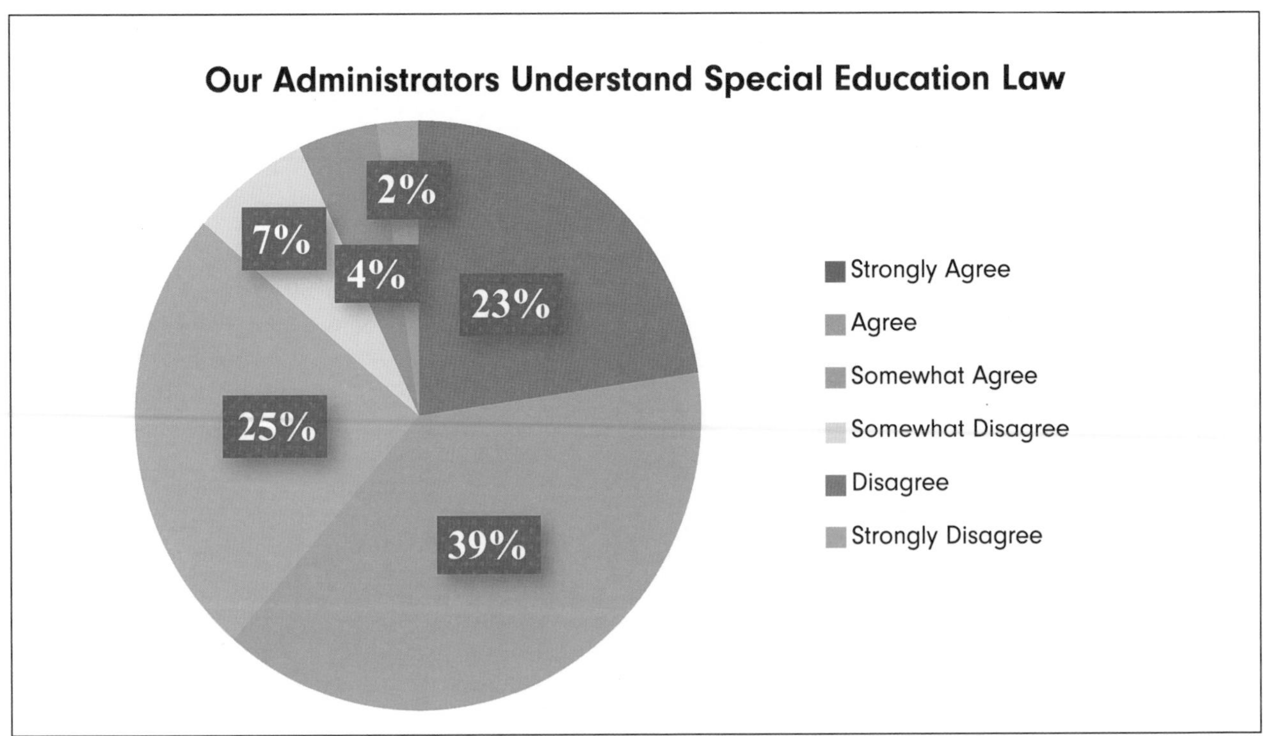

Figure 6.21: Principal Report of Teacher Understanding of Special Education Law

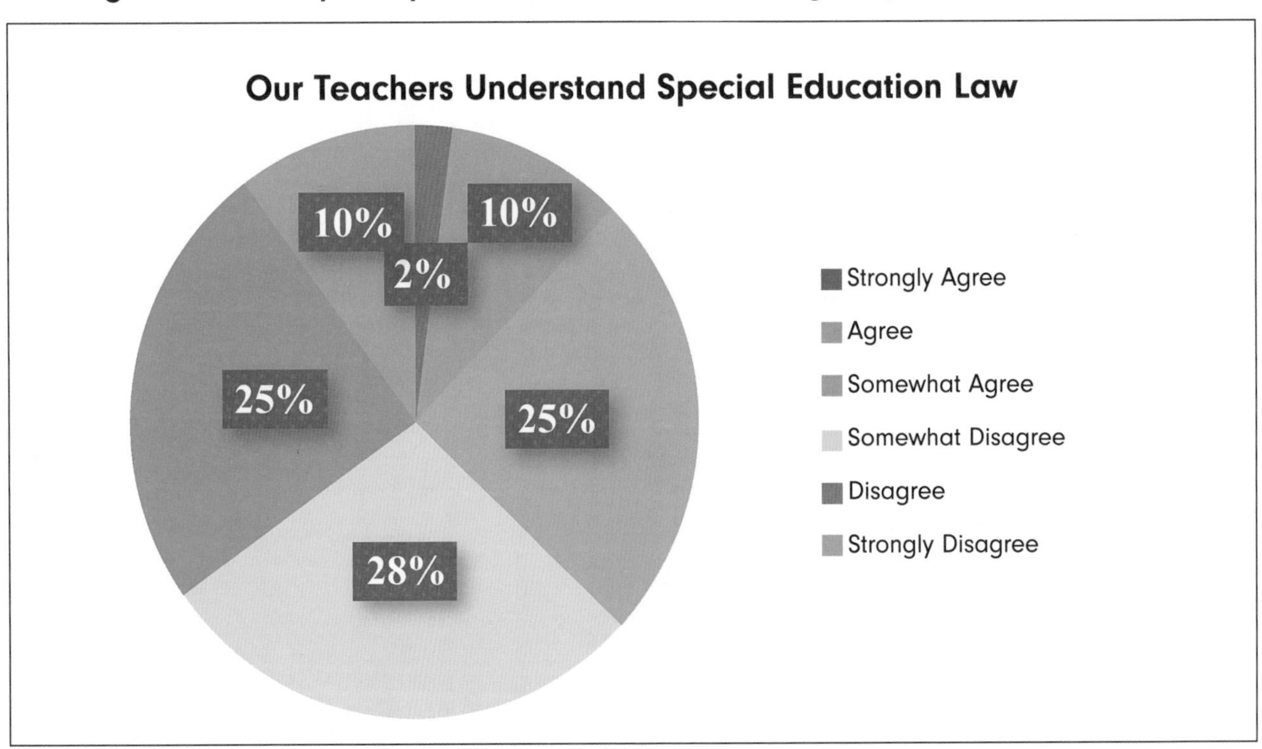

Figure 6.22: Principal Report of Teacher Understanding the Connection Between Disabilities and Learning

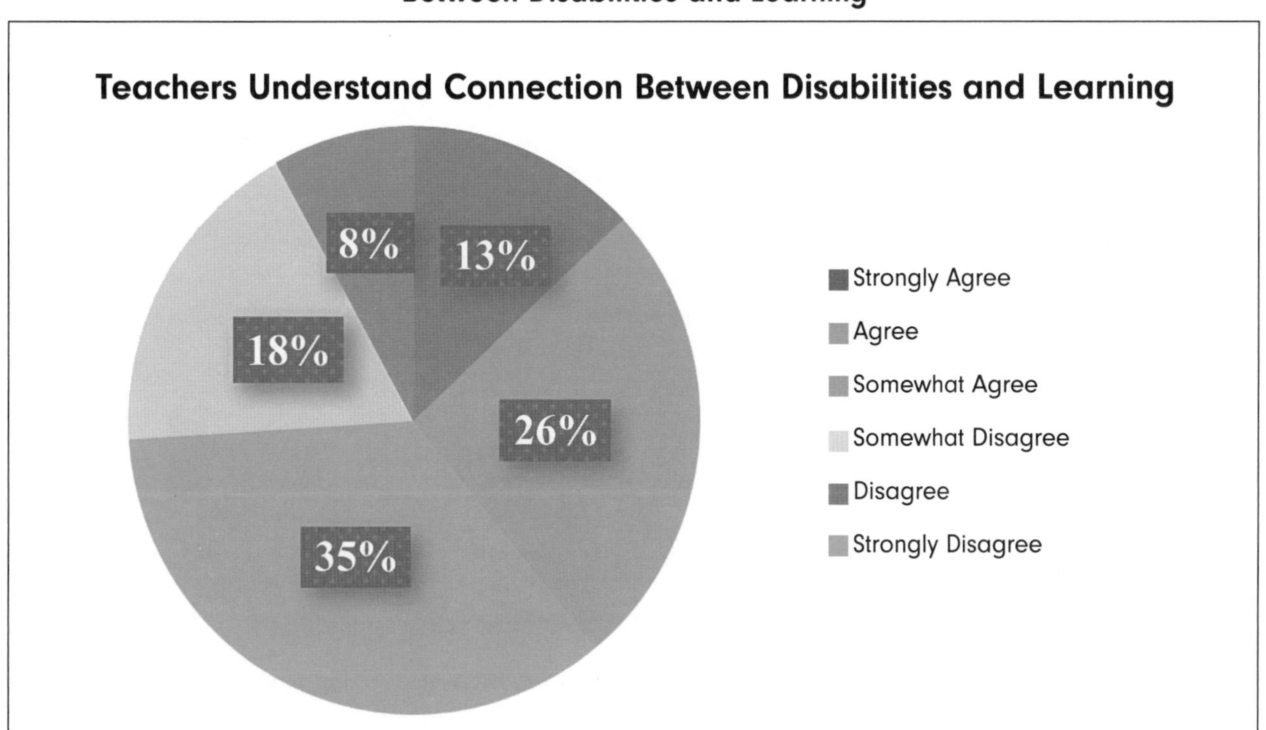

Attitudes and Dispositions

Principals were asked a series of attitudinal questions regarding educating their students with disabilities. The questions tackled four different areas: school responsibility, school environment, collaboration, and resources. Items were evaluated to determine if grade school and high school principals differed in their responses. No significant differences were found. Overall, principals reported that it is the responsibility of the private schools to educate students with disabilities and that this should not fall to the public schools (see Figure 6.23). They reported an attitude of inclusiveness regarding the teachers, administrators and non-disabled students toward their students with disabilities (see Figure 6.24). They also reported, in general, that parents are inclusive of students with disabilities; however, comparatively, parents' level of inclusivity was not as strong as those in the school.

Figure 6.23: Principal Report of Public/Private Schools' Responsibility to Educate Students with Disabilities

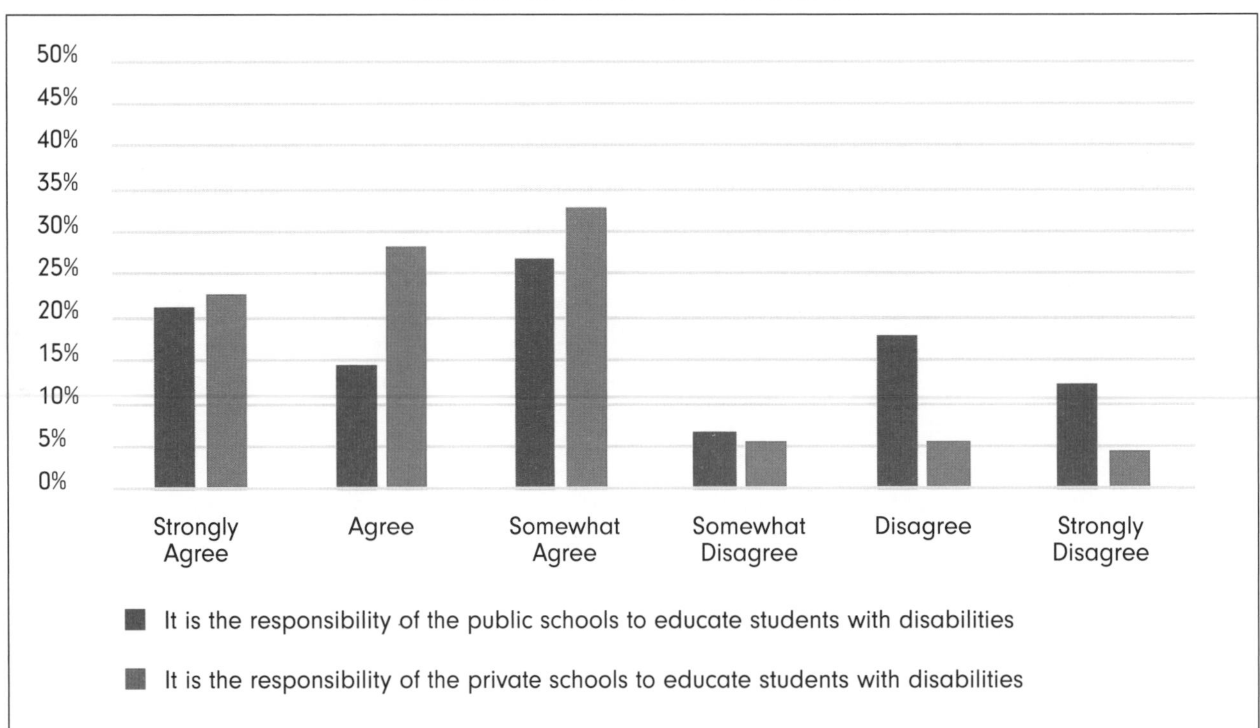

Figure 6.24: Principal Report of Attitudes of Inclusiveness of Students with Disabilities

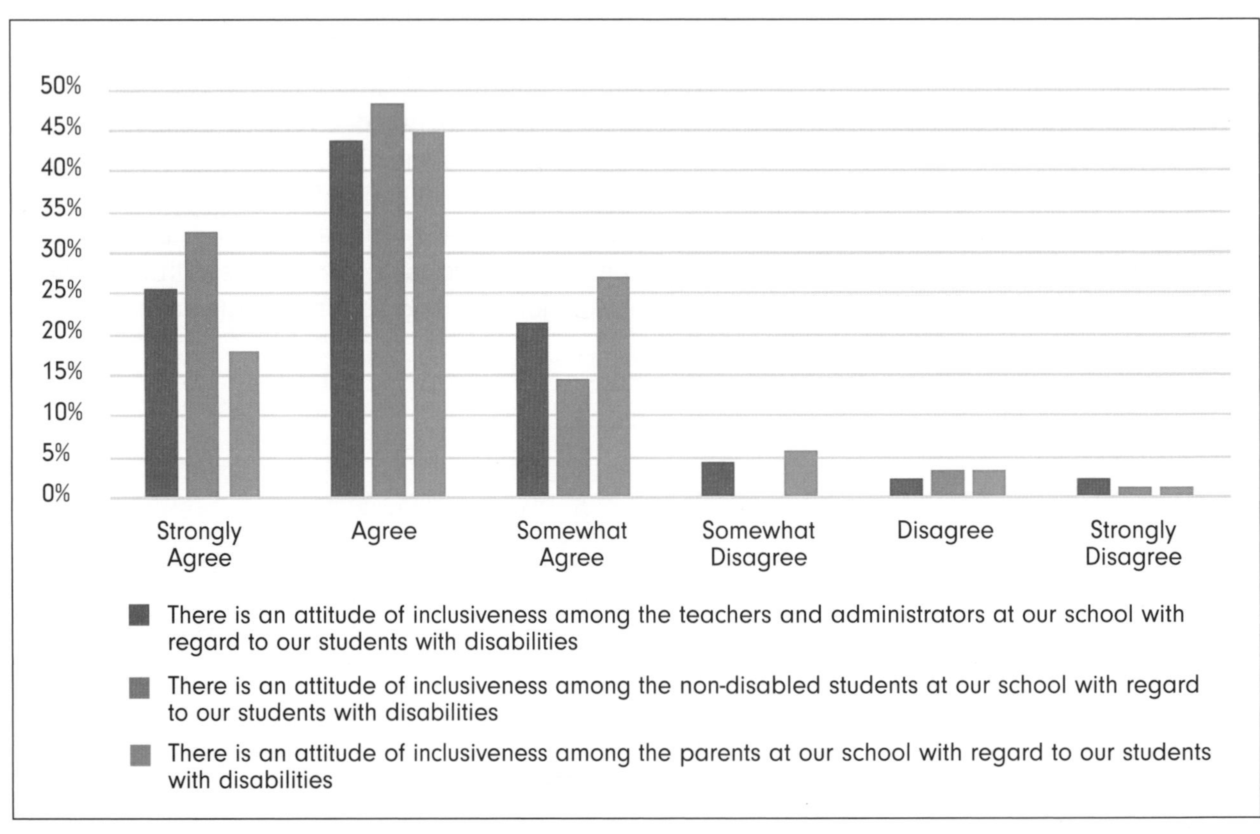

Regarding collaboration (see Figure 6.25) among the Catholic schools, there does seem to be some room for improvement. While the majority of the principals report sharing ideas and best practices regarding student disability programming with other Catholic schools, over one-third disagree that the diocesan office is helping to facilitate collaboration among the schools and with LEA.

Figure 6.25: Principal Perception of School Collaboration

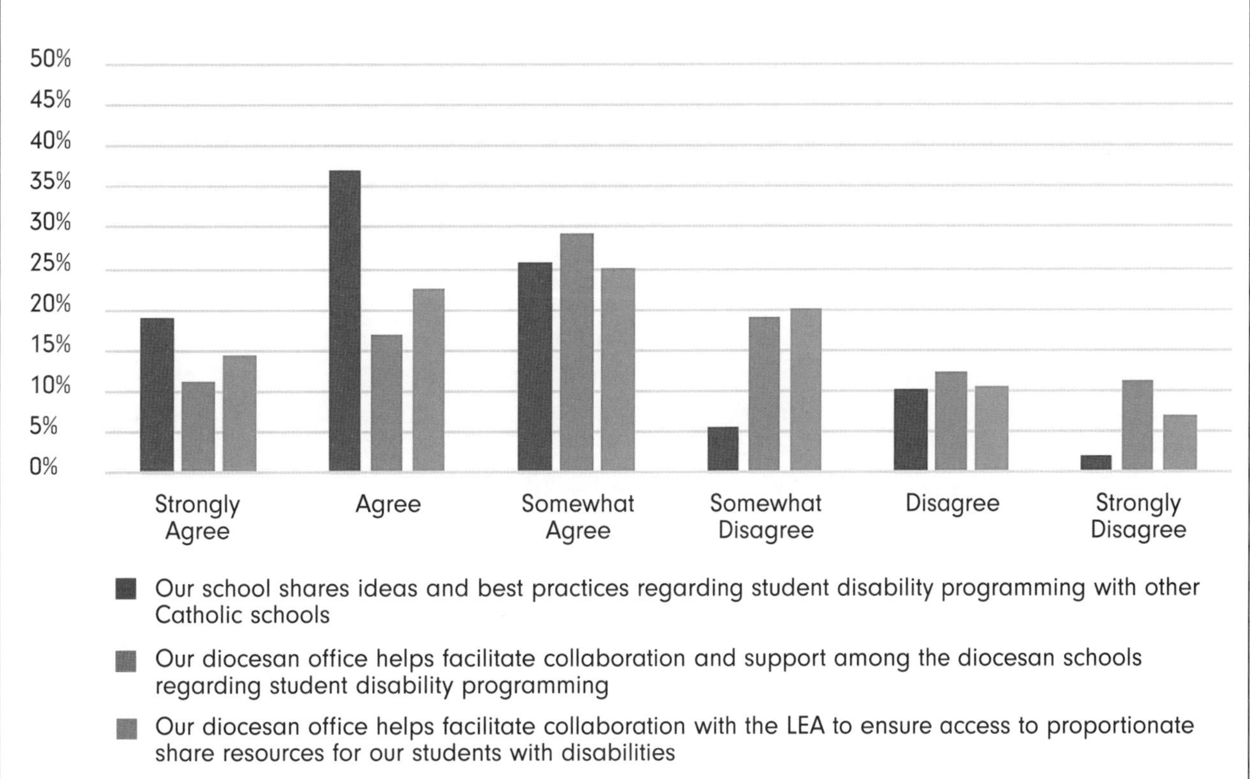

Superintendents' Final Thoughts

Superintendents were asked a few open-ended questions regarding their perceptions of promising practices in meeting the needs of students with disabilities, what they believe are the most pervasive challenges, and what they feel needs to be done to better deliver a Catholic education to students with disabilities. Promising practices were specific and varied, but a few common themes emerged. Programs that targeted a specific disability (e.g., autism) were mentioned by several superintendents, as were targeted schools or "schools within a school" to serve the population. Many, however, also mentioned cultural changes have created a positive shift. One superintendent wrote,

> *"Based partially on feedback from parents of students with disabilities, some examples of promising practices in our schools include creating a welcoming presence, a we-can-do-this attitude, and fostering an atmosphere of inclusion and belonging. Some of this may be due to an increased awareness of disabilities in our schools and how the student is affected by his or her disability. Other promising practices include more differentiation of instruction, smaller class sizes and advocates for children, teachers, and principals as well as increased support from the local public schools."*

By far, the greatest challenge they reported was a resource challenge - funding, time, personnel, but mostly, funding. One superintendent summarized the feelings by writing,

> *"[The challenges are] time and money. Our office consists of myself (superintendent), an assistant superintendent and an administrative assistant. We don't have the expertise or manpower to work individually with schools. Our schools work with nearly 40 different, public school districts. Everyone currently is struggling to understand and implement ESSA, and every public district has a different interpretation. We can't keep abreast of everything that is or isn't happening in each district. We also do not have anyone to write grants; nor do we have specific endowments established to address this need. Also, our diocese is mostly rural/suburban. The largest number of schools we have in a single, public school district is six. This means that we are unable to pool Title I and IDEA funds to hire third party service providers. We are generally at the mercy of the public school districts and what they do or don't offer. Also, it is difficult to give our principals a comprehensive understanding of the law so they can be good advocates during their consultations with public districts."*

Finally, the superintendents offered actionable items they believe will help in delivering a better Catholic education to more students with disabilities. The suggestions included changes to the mindset and establishing a real commitment to serving this population, greater collaboration among interested parties, more and better resources, and continuing professional development for teachers and administrators. One superintendent summarized all of this,

> *"We have to be committed to developing inclusive Catholic schools. We need to be tireless in seeking out high quality, on-going PD for all employees in our schools. We need to seek out new funding sources to assist where necessary. We need to develop strong, collaborative partnerships with our Catholic universities to align needs back to various educational programs. We need to tell our stories and celebrate the GOOD NEWS! We need to welcome families from all walks of life because that is our Gospel call and what truly makes authentic Catholic schools."*

Chapter 7

Next Steps

This inaugural survey was created in order to benchmark the current status of programs and services for addressing the needs of students with disabilities in the Catholic school setting. The survey was designed to assess four areas:

- Demographics
- Policies, Procedures and Protocols
- Services
- Challenges and Opportunities

Next Steps: Demographics – Whom Do We Serve?

The results of this survey are consistent with past assessments of this area. Catholic schools are continuing to enroll students with disabilities from a number of eligibility categories. The results suggest that the schools that responded to this survey tend to enroll students from high incidence disabilities categories (i.e. specific learning disabilities, other health impaired, and speech and language impairment). The respondents for this survey indicated that they were less likely to enroll students from low incidence categories (i.e. sensory impairments and intellectual disabilities). It may useful to explore the reasons why Catholic schools are admitting students with low incidence disabling conditions at lower rates. There may be some hesitancy in enrolling students with certain disability categories due to lack of experience. Boyle and Hernandez (2016) found that principals are more likely to enroll students with in some disability categories when the principal had past positive experience with individuals from those categories. Determining the reason may help to craft an appropriate system response to increase admissions rates of these students. This can serve to identify the necessary training components for future Catholic school leaders.

An interesting observation occurred in looking at the relationship between the number of minority students and the prevalence of students with disabilities. As suggested earlier, there is a correlation between the proportion of a school's population with a diagnosed disability and the proportion of the school's minority student population. As minority populations rise, so too does the percent of students with a diagnosed disability, except for schools with the greatest minority population. This observation should be framed with caution as the sample size was small, but this area may need further investigation to determine the prevailing rates. Additionally, because this relationship is correlational, causation is not implied. However, further investigation may be required in order to determine that minority students are not being over-identified with disabilities.

Next Steps: Policies, Procedures and Protocols

Three quarters of the superintendents noted that there were policies about students with disabilities in Catholic schools. However, only one-third of the respondent superintendents had specialized policy manuals devoted to this topic. Additionally, only one-third of the surveyed principals indicated that the school's handbook had policies about students with disabilities. It can't be enough to have willing teachers and dedicated leaders implement programing for students with disabilities. Policy helps to articulate the response to requests for services. Procedures concretize the policy in observable steps, and protocols are the concrete products through which the policy is realized. Creating a repository of model policies, procedures, and protocols can help identify promising models to assist other Catholic schools who may lack the resources to create these on their own.

It was interesting to note that schools tended to use universal screeners and discipline records at lower rates than other assessment tools to diagnose potential disability. These sources can be helpful in the evaluation of potential disability. It would be interesting to note if schools don't have access to universal screeners or to determine if there other reasons why these are not being utilized to a greater extent. Further, it would be important to find out how Catholic schools are maintaining discipline records and tracking that data in an on-going fashion. Again, this can be a very practical data source that is useful, not only in disability determination, but in shaping positive behavioral supports for all students.

In reviewing the results of the survey, there appears to be some needed work in the area of advocacy. Principals reported that they viewed accessing disability determination services through the public school as cumbersome. There might be a need to review local Catholic school procedures to work on a seamless interface with the public school child find process. Additionally, equipping Catholic school leaders with additional background in special education law can provide the basis for more effective advocacy.

Next Steps: Services

It is clear that the principals in this sample are reporting a wide variety of services for students with disabilities. It is also noteworthy that the respondents indicated that most of these services were provided for by the school budget as opposed to other sources.

Several interesting findings were noted in examining the survey data related to student outcomes. In the earlier grades, more progress in reading and math for students with learning disabilities and intellectual disabilities were noted in schools where supports and professional development were provided. Unfortunately, the progress was not as remarkable for those students with autism. This is not to say that students with autism can't make progress in Catholic schools. It is important to further investigate this dimension to identify the conditions which would facilitate more academic growth for students in this eligibility category. The lack of change in academic growth at the high school level cannot be attributed to presence or absences there of supports. The sample size did not allow for a robust statistical analysis of this factor for the high school level. Clearly, further investigation in this area is critical to find the right levels of supports for students with disabilities at the high school level.

Additionally, some of the positive outcomes in student achievement were correlated with the presence of certain types of professional development. Positive relationships were also noted for certain kinds of supports that were present in these schools. Again, this is important to note but further investigation is required to provide more in depth analysis.

Funding always seems to be the critical issue when discussing providing services for students with disabilities in Catholic schools. The results of this survey suggest that this sample of principals are finding channels to provide these services within their school budget. However, it is important that this issue be explored further. With budgetary concerns always at the fore and the continuing challenges interfacing with the local educational agencies, financial constraints will continue to present as a concern. It would seem that fostering in-depth discussion about how to balance the call to provide Catholic education to all who desire it and the requirement to manage fiscally responsible programs is needed at this juncture. As the U.S. bishops remind us,

> Costs must never be the controlling consideration limiting the welcome offered to those among us with disabilities, since provision of access to religious functions is a pastoral duty (USCCB, 1998, p.2).

The ultimate question is how to balance this charge with the very real financial concerns that face the Catholic school principal. It would seem that bringing together a forum for Catholic school staff, diocesan leaders, national organizations, universities and various foundations might help to begin the discussion.

Next Steps: Challenges and Opportunities

An interesting finding is related to connecting disability services to Catholic social teaching. Only about half of the principals indicated that their teachers and administrators received professional development in this area. The Church has a number of documents related to this, and they would seem the logical fit to provide the context for serving students with disabilities within this framework. Connecting this level of programming to Catholic identity provides the "why" to staff and is the perfect starting point. It seems that it would be critical to offer formation opportunities for staff and administrators in this area. Being able to explore various Church documents related to disability might provide a mindset change in the quest to develop this level of understanding.

Another opportunity exists in the provision of professional development opportunities for Catholic school teachers and administrators. Certainly, further development in the area of knowledge, skills, and dispositions for both teachers and administrators would help to build the capacity of staff to work effectively with students with disabilities.

The results of this survey suggest that there is a general level of agreement that Catholic schools should be providing levels of programming for students with disabilities. This seems to be more evident within school staff perceptions and not as developed for parents. It seems to be an important point for Catholic schools to consider. In addition to having consensus building opportunities for staff, the Catholic school should consider how they are engaging other stakeholders in this process.

Final Thoughts

The results of this survey are an interesting starting point. The results certainly suggest the need for frequent and on-going assessment in these areas of serving students with disabilities in Catholic Schools. It would seem that on-going assessments of areas of attitudes and dispositions might be important to document shifts in this kind of thinking. Additionally, on-going assessments of these areas might help to identify changes in programming, especially in direct programming and services to students, as well as important professional development to staff and administrators.

Increasing the number of respondents, especially the principal respondents, could help to develop a more comprehensive picture of the state of the field of special education services within the Catholic school setting. Additionally, increased completion of surveys from both principals and superintendents would provide more data for richer and more complex levels of analysis that ultimately could yield more recommendations for the field.

The results of this survey suggest that Catholic schools are taking seriously their call to begin to open their doors to all who desire a Catholic education. However, there is more work to be done in this area. Clearly, there is a need to continue to build the capacity of the leaders and staff of Catholic schools to address a wider range of student need. Better developed systems of advocacy at the local school level can help Catholic school leaders to better navigate the current systems of special education available in the public school sector.

It is heartening to see the positive attitudes towards serving students with disabilities in Catholic schools. Of the respondents, a majority indicated that there is a need for Catholic schools to embrace this responsibility to serve. Hopefully, the results of this survey have highlighted some of the promising shifts in thinking and in programming for students with disabilities. To echo the words of one of the responding superintendents,

> *...We need to tell our stories and celebrate the GOOD NEWS! We need to welcome families from all walks of life because that is our Gospel call and what truly makes authentic Catholic schools.*

Catholic schools must continue to share the good news of all that is being done to educate students with disabilities. Through continued work in this area, Catholic schools can heed the bishops' call, originally stated in the *Pastoral Statement of U.S. Catholic Bishops on People with Disabilities*, to welcome and, ultimately, to re-affirm their own Catholic identity.

References

Behrmann, E. H. (Ed.). (1971). *Catholic Special Education.* St. Louis, MO: B. Herder Book Co.

Bello, D. A. (2006). *The Status of Special Education Services in Catholic High Schools: Attributes, Challenges, and Needs.* Council for Exceptional Children. 72(4), 461-481.

Bimonte, R. (2004). *Balance Sheet for Catholic Elementary Schools: 2003 Income and Expenses.* Washington, DC: National Catholic Educational Association.

Boazman, J. (2017). *The Meaning of Gifts and Talents: Framing the Elements for Flourishing.* Arlington, VA: National Catholic Educational Association.

Boyle, M. (2010). *Response to Intervention: A Blueprint for Catholic Schools.* Arlington VA: National Catholic Educational Association.

Boyle, M. and Bernards, P. (2017). *One Spirit, One Body: An Agenda for Serving Students with Disabilities in Catholic Schools.* Arlington, VA: National Catholic Educational Association.

Boyle, M. J. & Hernandez, C. M. (2016). *An Investigation of the Attitudes of Catholic School Principals Towards the Inclusion of Students with Disabilities.* Journal of Catholic Education, 20 (1). Retrieved from: http://dx.doi. org/10.15365/joce.2001092016

Dees, J., Lichon, K., & and Roach, C. (2017). *Our Legacy and Our Future: A Framework for Serving English Language Learners in Catholic Schools.* Arlington, VA: National Catholic Educational Association.

DeFiore, L. (1999, Spring). *Special Needs Students Bring Gifts to Classrooms and Catechetical Centers.* National Apostolate Quarterly, 5-6.

DeFiore, L. (2001, January). *Assisting Children with Special Needs in Catholic Schools.* Paper presented at Making Room For Me Seminar 2001: Inclusion Through Collaborative Practices, Tampa, FL.

DeFiore, L. (2006). *The State of Special Education in Catholic Schools.* Journal of Catholic Education, 9 (4). Retrieved from http://digitalcommons.lmu.edu/ce/vol9/iss4/10

Dudek, A. (1998). *Is There Room for Me?* Washington, DC: National Catholic Educational Association.

Dudek, A. (2000). *Making Room for Me – Including Children with Special Needs [Special section].* Momentum, 31(2), 43-47.

Dudek, A. (personal communication) (2001). In Weaver, H. R., and Landers, M. F. (2002). *Serving Students with Special Needs in Catholic Schools*, in T. C. Hunt, E. A. Joseph, and R. J. Nuzzi (Eds.), Catholic Schools Still Make a Difference; Ten Years of Research, 1991-2000 (pp. 117-130). Washington, DC: National Catholic Educational Association.

Guerra, M. J. (1998). *CHS 2000: A First Look.* Washington, DC: National Catholic Educational Association.

Hall, S.E. & Dudek, A. (Eds.). (1987b). *Special Education in the Future.* Special Education, 8(3), 1-2.

Haney, R., & O'Keefe, J. M. (1998). *Providing for the Diverse Needs of Youth and Their Families: Conversations in Excellence.* Washington, DC: National Catholic Educational Association.

Hunt, T. C., Joseph, E. A. & Nuzzi, R. J. (2002). *Catholic Schools Still Make A Difference: Ten Years of Research 1991-2000.* Washington, DC: National Catholic Educational Association.

Kealey, R. J. (1996). *Balance Sheet for Catholic Elementary Schools: 1995 Income and Expenses.* Washington, DC: National Catholic Educational Association.

Kealey, R. J. (1998). *Balance Sheet for Catholic Elementary Schools: 1997 Income and Expenses.* Washington, DC: National Catholic Educational Association.

Kealey, R. J. (2000). *Balance Sheet for Catholic Elementary Schools: 1999 Income and Expenses.* Washington, DC: National Catholic Educational Association.

Lia, M. (2017). *Core Reading Instruction.* Arlington, VA: National Catholic Educational Association.

McDonald, D., & Schultz, M. (2016). *United States Catholic Elementary and Secondary Schools: 2015-2016.* Arlington, VA: National Catholic Educational Association.

McDonald, D., & Schultz, M. (2017). *United States Catholic Elementary and Secondary Schools: 2016-2017.* Arlington, VA: National Catholic Educational Association.

National Catholic Educational Association. (1999). *A Reflection Statement on Inclusion.* Washington, DC. Author.

National Catholic Educational Association (2017). *Who Are Exceptional Learners in Catholic Schools?* Arlington, VA. Author.

United States Catholic Conference. (1978). *Pastoral Statement of U.S. Catholic Bishops on People with Disabilities.* Washington, DC: Author.

United States Catholic Conference of Catholic Bishops (1998). *Welcome and Justice for Persons with Disabilities: A Framework of Access and Inclusion.* Washington, DC: Author.

United States Conference of Catholic Bishops. (2002b). *Catholic School Children with Disabilities.* Washington, DC: Author.

U.S. Department of Education, National Center for Education Statistics, Schools and Staffing Survey (SASS), "Public School and Private School Data Files," 2011–12.

Weaver, H. R., & Landers, M. F. (2002). *Serving Students with Special Needs in Catholic Schools.* In T. C. Hunt, E. A. Joseph, & R. J. Nuzzi (Eds.), *Catholic Schools Still Make a Difference: Ten Years of Research, 1991-2000* (pp. 117-130). Washington, DC: National Catholic Educational Association.

Appendix A

Exceptional Learners in Catholic Schools Benchmark Survey: Principal Version

School Demographics:

1. In what NCEA region is your school located?
2. In what type of community is your school located?
    a. Urban
    b. Inner City
    c. Suburban
    d. Rural
3. Is your school…
    a. Parish
    b. Interparish
    c. Diocesan
    d. Congregation
    e. Network
4. What grades does your school service? ______________________________
5. What is your *total* student enrollment? ______________________________
6. How many of your students comprise the following racial groups?
    a. America Indian/Native American N= ______________________________
    b. Asian N = ______________________________
    c. Black N= ______________________________
    d. Native Hawaiian/Pacific Islander N= ______________________________

e. Multiracial N=______

f. White N=______

g. Unknown N= ______

7. How many of your students comprise the following ethnic groups?

   a. Hispanic/Latino N=______

   b. Non-Hispanic/Latino N=______

8. How many of your students are non-Catholic? N= ______

9. Does your school require information about a potential student's disabilities as part of the application process?

   a. Yes

   b. No

10. How many of your students have a *diagnosed* disability? N=______

11. How many of your students with a disability were diagnosed *after* enrollment in your school? N= ______

12. In the last year, have you tracked the number of students with a disability who are identified through Child Find?

    a. Yes

    b. No

13. How many of your students with a disability *who are diagnosed after enrollment* in your school are initially identified through Child Find? N= ______

14. What is the total number of current students at your school who have been diagnosed with the following disabilities:

    a. Specific learning disability/SLD (e.g., dyslexia, dysgraphia) N=______

    b. Other health impairment (e.g., ADHD) N=______

    c. Autism spectrum disorder (ASD) N= ______

    d. Emotional disturbance (e.g., anxiety, schizophrenia, OCD) N= ______

    e. Speech or language impairment N= ______

    f. Visual impairment, including blindness N=______

    g. Deafness N= ______

    h. Hearing impairment (Note: auditory processing disorder is covered under specific learning disorder) N=______

i. Deaf-blindness N= ______________________________

j. Orthopedic impairment (e.g., cerebral palsy) N= ______________________________

k. Intellectual disability (e.g., down syndrome) N= ______________________________

l. Traumatic brain injury N= ______________________________

Identification of Disabilities / Referrals

15. Does your school use any of the following to determine if a student has a *suspected* disability?

	Yes	No	I don't know
Standardized tests			
Universal Screening			
Benchmark Tests			
Classroom performance			
Discipline record			
Classroom observations			
Psychological evaluation			

16. Are there students that you suspect have a disability yet are undiagnosed? (Please *do not include* students who are currently going through a referral/diagnostic process)

    a. Yes

    b. No (skip to #18)

17. Indicate how much you agree or disagree that each of the following contribute to why the students have not yet been diagnosed?

	Strongly Agree	Agree	Somewhat Agree	Somewhat Disagree	Disagree	Strongly Disagree
Not part of overall Catholic school program						
Process with the public school is too cumbersome						
Process with the Catholic school is too cumbersome						
Parents are resistant						
Cost						
Concerns of stigma						

Other ______________________________

18. Does your school have a written referral policy to refer students with suspected disabilities for further testing?

a. Yes

b. No

19. In a Response to Intervention (RtI) Model, does your school require Tier I and Tier II Interventions before a student is referred for a comprehensive evaluation?

a. Yes

b. No

c. Have not implemented RtI

20. In an academic year, on average, what percentage of referrals for disability testing are initiated by the following:

a. Parents ______________ %

b. Classroom teacher ______________ %

c. Social service ______________ %

d. Special needs teacher ______________ %

e. Other ______________ %

f. Other (please list) ______________________________

Evaluation / Testing

21. On average, what percent of your students *who are suspected of having a disability* are referred to *public school evaluators* for their initial evaluation? ____________________ %

    a. On average, what percent of those students who are referred to a public school evaluator are found to have a disability? ____________% (If you do not have this information, please mark NA)

22. On average, what percent of your students *who are suspected of having a disability* are referred to *a private evaluator* for their initial evaluation? ________________________ %

    a. On average, of those who are referred to a private evaluator, what percent are found to have a disability? __________% (If you do not have this information, please mark NA)

Provision of Services

23. For each, please indicate if your school would admit/serve a student with the *known disability*? (*Select one response for each disability type*)

	Yes, we would admit them – no exceptions	We may admit them depending on the severity of the disability	No, we would not admit them after diagnosis, *but* we would work with a student if they were diagnosed *after* admission	No, we would not admit them and could not provide services if they were diagnosed *after* admission
Specific learning disability/SLD (e.g., dyslexia, dysgraphia)				
Other health impairment (e.g., ADHD)				
Autism spectrum disorder (ASD)				
Emotional disturbance (e.g., anxiety, schizophrenia, OCD)				
Speech or language impairment				
Visual impairment, including blindness				
Deafness				
Hearing impairment (Note: auditory processing disorder is covered under specific learning disorder)				
Deaf-blindness				
Orthopedic impairment (e.g., cerebral palsy)				
Intellectual disability (e.g., down syndrome)				
Traumatic brain injury				
Multiple disabilities				

24. Describe the process for considering a student with a mobility disability to be enrolled in your school.

25. Describe the process for considering a student with a sensory (hearing and vision) disability to be enrolled in your school.

26. Describe the process for considering a student with a cognitive disability to be enrolled in your school.

27. Describe how you would incorporate parent participation in the plan development for a child with a disability.

28. Does your school have written policies regarding how to include students with disabilities into the school? ______________________________

    a. Yes

    b. No

29. Does your school offer the following special education services? If your school does not offer the service, please indicate the *primary* reason it is not offered from the options below.

	Yes	No, it is too expensive	No, we do not have the personnel	No, we do not have the physical space	No, it is not needed
Resource Support					
Co-Teaching					
Inclusion					
Self-contained special education classroom					
Speech and Language Services					
Occupational Therapy					
Physical Therapy					
School Psychologist					
Counseling Support					
Nurse					
Paraprofessionals					

30. Are there other services your school offers that are not listed above?

31. Are there other services your school *would like to offer but doesn't* that are not listed above? Please explain why they are not offered.

32. How accessible is your school for students with…

	Accessible	Somewhat Accessible	Inaccessible
Mobility Impairments			
Sensory (hearing and vision) Impairments			
Cognitive Disability			

Funding

33. We would like to know how your special education services are funded. For each, please indicate the percent that is provided by LEA/proportionate plan, by the school and by parent's insurance.

a. How much of the funding for *resource support* is provided by… (If your school does not offer the service, please mark NA.)

i. Provided by the school _______________%

ii. Provided by the parent or parent's insurance _______________%

iii. Provided by LEA/proportionate plan _______________%

iv. Provided by "other" _______________%

b. How much of the funding for *co-teaching* is provided by… (If your school does not offer the service, please mark NA.)

i. Provided by the school _______________%

ii. Provided by the parent or parent's insurance _______________%

iii. Provided by LEA/proportionate plan _______________%

iv. Provided by "other" _______________%

c. How much of the funding for *inclusion* is provided by… (If your school does not offer the service, please mark NA.)

i. Provided by the school _______________%

ii. Provided by the parent or parent's insurance _______________%

iii. Provided by LEA/proportionate plan _______________%

iv. Provided by "other" _______________%

d. How much of the funding for *self-contained special education classrooms* is provided by... (If your school does not offer the service, please mark NA.)

i. Provided by the school ________________%

ii. Provided by the parent or parent's insurance ______________%

iii. Provided by LEA/proportionate plan ______________%

iv. Provided by "other" _________________%

e. How much of the funding for *speech and language services* is provided by... (If your school does not offer the service, please mark NA.)

i. Provided by the school ________________%

ii. Provided by the parent or parent's insurance ______________%

iii. Provided by LEA/proportionate plan ______________%

iv. Provided by "other" _________________%

f. How much of the funding for *occupational therapy* is provided by... (If your school does not offer the service, please mark NA.)

i. Provided by the school ________________%

ii. Provided by the parent or parent's insurance ______________%

iii. Provided by LEA/proportionate plan ______________%

iv. Provided by "other" _________________%

g. How much of the funding for *counseling support* is provided by... (If your school does not offer the service, please mark NA.)

i. Provided by the school ________________%

ii. Provided by the parent or parent's insurance ______________%

iii. Provided by LEA/proportionate plan ______________%

iv. Provided by "other" _________________%

h. How much of the funding for a *nurse(s)* is provided by... (If your school does not offer the service, please mark NA.)

i. Provided by the school ________________%

ii. Provided by the parent or parent's insurance ______________%

iii. Provided by LEA/proportionate plan ______________%

iv. Provided by "other" _________________%

i. How much of the funding for *paraprofessionals* is provided by... (If your school does not offer the service, please mark NA.)

i. Provided by the school ________________%

ii. Provided by the parent or parent's insurance _______________%

iii. Provided by LEA/proportionate plan _______________%

iv. Provided by "other" _________________%

34. If you indicated above that some of your special education sources are funded by "other" sources, please list the additional funding sources.

35. Has your school sought funding through outside agencies/grant organizations to help cover the cost of education for your disabled student population?

a. Yes

b. No

36. How many students are dually enrolled with LEA in order to access services? ___________

37. Do you or your representative attend the Timely and Meaningful Consultation meeting where the proportionate plans are developed?

a. Yes

b. No

38. How satisfied or dissatisfied are you with the proportionate plans that are developed?

a. Very satisfied

b. Satisfied

c. Somewhat satisfied

d. Somewhat dissatisfied

e. Dissatisfied

f. Very dissatisfied

39. Please describe any concerns that you have with the Timely and Meaningful Consultation process and the Proportionate Plan development.

Assessment

40. Does your school track the effectiveness of interventions used with your students with disabilities?

a. Yes

b. No

41. Please describe the method your school uses to track the effectiveness of interventions used with your students with disabilities. <<open ended>>

Professional Development

42. Are administrators and/or teachers in your school offered the following professional development opportunities that may assist them in working with students with disabilities? (Select a response for each PD opportunity)

	Offered to *both teachers and administrators*	Offered to *teachers only*	Offered to *administrators only*	*Not offered* to teachers or administrators
Understanding various disabilities and the interference they have with learning				
Classroom skills and strategies that may be useful in working with students with disabilities (e.g., differentiation of instruction, co-teaching)?				
Developing accommodations and modifications to assist students with disabilities				
Understanding special education law				
Positive behavioral management strategies				
Connection between Catholic Social Teaching and serving students with disabilities				
Response to Intervention/Multi-tiered Systems of Support (RtI/MTSS) framework				

Attitudinal Questions

43. How much do you agree or disagree with the following:

	Strongly Agree	Agree	Somewhat Agree	Somewhat Disagree	Disagree	Strongly Disagree
It is the responsibility of *public schools* to educate students with disabilities.						
It is the responsibility of *private schools* to educate students with disabilities.						
There is an attitude of inclusiveness among the teachers and administrators at our school with regard to our students with disabilities.						
There is an attitude of inclusiveness among the non-disabled students at our school with regard to our students with disabilities.						
There is an attitude of inclusiveness among the parents at our school with regard to our students with disabilities.						
Our school shares ideas and best practices regarding student disability programming with other Catholic schools.						
Our diocesan office helps facilitate collaboration and support among the diocesan schools regarding student disability programming.						

Continued on next page

	Strongly Agree	Agree	Somewhat Agree	Somewhat Disagree	Disagree	Strongly Disagree
Our diocesan office helps facilitate collaboration with the LEA to ensure access to proportionate share resources for our students with disabilities.						
Our teachers have a strong understanding of the connection between various disabilities and learning.						
Our teachers have effective skills for working with students with disabilities.						
Our *teachers* understand the special education law.						
Our *administrators* understand the special education law.						
Our school has effective assessment practices to use in assessing growth among our disabled student population.						
Our *teachers* have a firm understanding of the Response to Intervention/ Multi-tiered Systems of Support (RtI/MTSS) framework.						
Our *administrators* have a firm understanding of the Response to Intervention/ Multi-tiered Systems of Support (RtI/MTSS) framework.						
Our *teachers* have a firm understanding of root cause analysis.						
Our *administrators* have a firm understanding of root cause analysis.						

The next set of questions asks about the academic growth of your students with disabilities. We understand that progress is very individual and often times difficult to measure across a group. Part of our undertaking with this study is to better understand the relationship between institutional policies and practices and student outcomes so that we can recognize what works well and share that information with our schools. This *final* set of questions should take no more than 3-5 minutes to complete and is crucial to our ability to tie practices with outcomes.

44. Please tell us again so we can direct you to the appropriate questions, which of the following grades does your school include?

    a. K-8

    b. 9-12

45. Does your school have any students who are disabled in grades K-3?

    a. Yes

    b. No

46. ***Compared*** *to the start of the 2015-16* academic year, **on average**, how would you describe the *reading abilities* of your students with a disability in grades K-2 *at the end of the 2015-16 academic year?*

	N/A – We don't have any K-3 students with this disability	Much stronger	Stronger	No change	Weaker	Much weaker
Reading ability for students with an ***intellectual/cognitive disability***						
Reading ability for students with a ***learning disability***						
Reading ability for students with ***autism***						

47. What measures are used to determine change in ability of the student?

	Yes	No	I don't know
Standardized testing			
Benchmark Assessments (DIBELS, AIMSWeb, MAP, STAR, etc.)			
Classroom performance			
Classroom observations			
Discipline records			

48. Does your school have any students who are disabled in grades 4-8?

a. Yes

b. No

49. Compared to the start of the 2015-16 academic year, ***on average***, how would you describe the *reading and math abilities* of your students with a disability in grades 5-8 at the end of the 2015-16 academic year?

	N/A – We don't have any 4-8 students with this disability	Much stronger	Stronger	No change	Weaker	Much weaker
Reading ability for students with an ***intellectual/cognitive disability***						
Reading ability for students with a ***learning disability***						
Reading ability for students with ***autism***						
Math ability for students with an ***intellectual/ cognitive disability***						
Math ability for students with a ***learning disability***						
Math ability for students with ***autism***						

50. What measures are used to determine change in ability of the student?

	Yes	No	I don't know
Standardized testing			
Benchmark Assessments (DIBELS, AIMSWeb, MAP, STAR, etc.)			
Classroom performance			
Classroom observations			
Discipline records			

Go to end of survey for those who answered this set of questions.

51. Does your school have any students who are disabled in grades 9-12?

a. Yes

b. No

52. Compared to the start of the 2015-16 academic year, ***on average***, how would you describe the *reading and math abilities* of your students with a disability in grades 9-12 at the end of the 2015-16 academic year?

	N/A – We don't have any 9-12 students with this disability	Much stronger	Stronger	No change	Weaker	Much weaker
Reading ability for students with an ***intellectual/cognitive disability***						
Reading ability for students with a ***learning disability***						
Reading ability for students with ***autism***						
Math ability for students with an ***intellectual/ cognitive disability***						
Math ability for students with a ***learning disability***						
Math ability for students with ***autism***						

53. What measures are used to determine change in ability of the student?

	Yes	No	I don't know
Standardized testing			
Benchmark Assessments			
Classroom performance			
Classroom observations			
Discipline records			

Appendix B

Exceptional Learners in Catholic Schools Benchmark Survey: Superintendent Version

School Demographics:

1. In what NCEA region is your school district located?
2. In what type of community is your school district located?
   a. Urban
   b. Inner City
   c. Suburban
   d. Rural
3. Is your school district…
   a. Parish
   b. Interparish
   c. Diocesan
   d. Congregation
   e. Network
4. What is your *total* student enrollment? ________________________________
5. How many of your students have a diagnosed disability? N=________________
6. Are there written policies in your diocesan handbook about the provision of services for students with disabilities?
   a. Yes
   b. No

7. Does your diocese have a separate handbook outlining common systems of support for meeting the needs of students with disabilities in diocesan schools?

   a. Yes

   b. No

8. Is there a designated person in the Office of Catholic Schools who is responsible for overseeing the delivery of services to students with disabilities in diocesan schools?

   a. Yes

   b. No

9. Does your diocese have a designated person in the Office of Catholic Schools who is responsible for overseeing the government programs related to delivery of service to students with disabilities in diocesan schools?

   a. Yes

   b. No

10. Describe how the Office of Catholic Schools in your diocese is involved in the development of proportionate share plans across the schools in your diocese

11. Does the *diocese provide* professional development opportunities that may assist teachers/administrators in working with students with disabilities? (Select a response for each PD opportunity.)

	Provided to *both teachers and administrators*	**Provided to *teachers only***	**Provided to *administrators only***	***Not offered* to teachers or administrators**
Provides PD to facilitate understanding of various disabilities and the interference they have with learning				
Provides PD regarding classroom skills and strategies that may be useful in working with students with disabilities (e.g., differentiation of instruction, co-teaching)?				
Provides PD in developing accommodations and modifications to assist students with disabilities				
Provides PD regarding understanding special education law				
Provides PD around positive behavioral management strategies				
Provides PD to help better understand the connection between Catholic Social Teaching and serving students with disabilities				
Provides PD regarding Response to Intervention/Multi-tiered Systems of Support (RtI/MTSS) framework				

12. Does the Office of Catholic Schools, in your diocese help parish schools find additional funding through grants and foundations to support serving students with disabilities?

    a. Yes

    b. No

13. Does the Office of Catholic Schools in your diocese seek formalized partnerships with colleges and universities to support the local diocesan schools in serving students with disabilities?

    a. Yes

    b. No

14. From the Office of Catholic Schools, what are some of the challenges that face the local Catholic schools when addressing the needs of students with disabilities?

15. In the schools in your diocese, what are some of the promising practices that you have observed in meeting the needs of students with disabilities?

16. In your view, what needs to happen in order to deliver a Catholic education to more students with disabilities?